BREAKTHROUGH

BREAKTHROUGH

Autobiographical Accounts of the Education
of Some Socially Disadvantaged Children

EDITED BY

RONALD GOLDMAN

LONDON
ROUTLEDGE & KEGAN PAUL

Published 1968
by Routledge & Kegan Paul Limited
Broadway House, 68-74 Carter Lane
London, E.C.4

Printed in Great Britain by
Clarke, Doble & Brendon Ltd
Cattedown, Plymouth

SBN 7100 6253 2

TO J. WHO INSPIRED
THIS BOOK

CONTENTS

CONTENTS

INTRODUCTION

The contributors to this volume have been invited to write about their educational breakthrough from a working-class beginning, an early slum environment, or both. All have attained some measure of success either in formal educational results or vocational achievement, despite unpromising beginnings as socially disadvantaged children. In writing these accounts they are not blowing their own trumpets, neither are they inviting the reader to marvel at their cleverness and strength of character. Indeed, I have had great difficulty in persuading them to commit to paper their experience. My sole intention as editor, and theirs as contributors, has been to supply autobiographical descriptions which might cast some light on the factors which have caused them to break through from limited and unpromising beginnings. Perhaps in so doing they have provided insights which educators, social workers, politicians and planners could use for the future in framing educational and social policies.

These accounts are of necessity subjective and highly interpretative. Coming as they do from those who have achieved some measure of success in higher education, politics, business, literature and the Arts and Sciences, they present very varied and moving descriptions. It is plain there is no one way of emerging from serious social disadvantage. There are many, and these routes out of the limitations of language, slum neighbourhoods, impoverished circumstances and social disadvantage may be more numerous than we think.

Lest some find in these accounts support for complacency, because 'those who have anything about them always get through', I would remind the reader that for every one who achieves a breakthrough there are tens of thousands who do not. Not only are those who remain impoverished—and this is not meant in an economic, but in an educational and cultural sense—but the nation also is impoverished at a time when we need all the human resources, talent and potential which can be released. There has been a great deal written about the best use of the nation's talents in educational and sociological reports in the past decade. A brief review of these writings, and the issues they raise, is a relevant context in which to set the autobiographies which form the rest of this volume.

In two educational reports[1] attention has been focused upon what is termed the increasing 'pool of ability'. More and more late adolescents look forward to the prospect of some form of higher education and are plainly capable of profiting from it. Society is in need of a greater number of those with increased training and higher qualifications, from the rank of technician through to teachers, administrators, scientists and higher levels of professional competence demanding greater ability and intelligence.

Despite the fact that gross numbers show an increase in the size of 'the pool of ability', some disquiet is expressed by educational and social investigators that the proportion of those contributing to the pool who come from working-class backgrounds are not increasing in proportion to their numbers. The increase comes mainly from those with a middle-class orientation or at least those families with middle-class aspirations. Jackson and Marsden[2] in their qualitative study of 88 working-class children in a northern industrial city illustrate in depth the wastage of talent from school, which the Crowther and Robbins Reports discuss, supported by national surveys. The wastage is very clearly seen at the top end of secondary schools where those from a limited social background, who have real ability, tend to leave much earlier than their middle-class peers.

Floud, Halsey and Martin[3] in a study of South West Hertfordshire and Middlesbrough reveal the social disadvantages of working-class boys in gaining grammar-school places. As

[1] *15-18* (The Crowther Report), London, H.M.S.O., 1959. *Higher Education* (The Robbins Report), London, H.M.S.O., 1963.

[2] Jackson, B. and Marsden, D., *Education and the Working-Class*, London, Routledge & Kegan Paul, 1962.

[3] Floud, J. E., Halsey, A. H., Martin, F. M., *Social Class and Educational Opportunity*, London, Heinemann, 1957.

they remark, 'The problem of equality of educational opportunity is now more complicated than when it took the simple form of the need to secure free access to grammar-schools on equal intellectual terms.' They continue, 'The need arises to understand the optimum conditions for the integration of school and home environment at all social levels in such a way as to minimize the educational disadvantages of both. . . .'

Another study by Douglas[4] has contributed to this disturbing picture by showing children from the manual working-class, suffering from striking disadvantages in primary-school performance as well as in using the wider opportunities of gaining grammar-school places. Douglas suggests that much of the wastage of ability seen in the working-class children he studied could be prevented by better teaching in primary schools, 'even if the attitude of working-class parents to education does not change'. But he goes much further in suggesting that it is in the pre-school years than many working-class children are stunted 'by the intellectual poverty of their surroundings'.

Children reared and educated in a restricted and limited area in central Liverpool have been the subject of detailed study by J. B. Mays[5]. The pupils of Crown Street schools set in a substandard and run-down area, described by the author, appear to be as good material educationally as any other section of the population. Yet they also appear to provide an outstanding example of the misfortune of the children in our society, of average and just above average ability, whose schooling now ends at fifteen years of age and for whom at that time education ends abruptly. Mays lists the cumulative disadvantages still suffered today by these children. They are physical shortcomings, poor buildings and inadequate school facilities, high turnover in staffing due to teachers becoming disheartened, the inertia of adults in the family and poor home stimulation and support for education, the innate capacity of some of the pupils and a high incidence of backwardness in school achievements, the local social milieu itself with its limiting loyalties, easy-

[4] Douglas, J. W. B., *The Home and the School*, London, MacGibbon & Kee, 1964.

[5] Mays, J. B., *Education and the Urban Child*, Liverpool University Press, 1962.

going hedonism, pursuit of short-term goals and strong prejudices against 'book-learning'. In another book[6] Mays describes some of the anti-social behaviour, costly to the community, which often accompanies social disadvantage.

These investigations are open to differing interpretations. What stands out clearly is the obvious disappointed response to the slogan of 'equality of opportunity' proclaimed so fervently in 1944. It may well be that it has remained only a slogan and that real equality of educational opportunity does not exist in our society. Can this equality be a reality where there are obvious inequalities of social opportunities? These inequalities are many, including poor slum neighbourhoods into which, even today in Britain, many millions of children are born, lack of early perceptual stimulation in the young, poor interest in education by parents, overcrowded schools and classes and shortage of teachers, and even the unequal distribution of grammar-school places in different parts of Britain.

The work of Basil Bernstein,[7] although still in its initial stages, has focused upon one area of deprivation closely tied to the social status and culture of the working-classes. Bernstein suggests that there exists two languages available to children. One is a 'public' language and the other is a 'formal' language. Among the characteristics of a public language are the use of short, grammatically simple, often unfinished sentences, simple and repetitive use of conjunctions, and an inability to hold a formal subject through a speech sequence. It is a language of implicit meanings and is extremely predictable and restricting in communication. On the other hand, a formal language is one in which the formal possibilities and syntax are much more flexible. Meaning is explicit and the speaker is able to make highly individual selection and permutation.

With a formal language the child is encouraged to think propositionally and abstractly, and in the language of education much earlier in a middle and upper-class home. This is not merely a matter of vocabulary but of a whole mode of

[6] Mays, J. B., *On the Threshold of Delinquency*, Liverpool University Press, 1959.

[7] Bernstein, B., *Social Structure, Language and Learning*, Educational Research, III, 3, June 1961.

communication, indicating different attitudes, ways of life and cultural emphasis. Where a child is confined only to a public language he may be unable to break through into a world which offers increasing educational opportunity, simply because he does not possess the necessary tools to seize the opportunities offered. When this is reinforced by poor parental attitudes to education, poor school achievements and the lure of well paid jobs which require little or no educational qualifications, we can understand the lack of motivation on the part of many who potentially could climb further up the educational ladders provided.

In 1963 an important educational commission called attention to the situation of those of average and below-average ability in our secondary schools.[8] A significant chapter in this report was that dealing with schools in problem and slum areas. Even in this affluent era in which we live the descriptions of the deficiencies of these schools, reflecting the deficiencies of the neighbourhoods in which they are placed, strike home in terms of their impact upon the children themselves. If 'the rich get richer and the poor get poorer' is not true economically any more, it does still appear to be true in terms of social disadvantage. Disadvantages tend to be cumulative, poor housing leading often to lack of playing space, inadequate provision of nursery schools, old decaying school buildings, overcrowded classes and a high turnover rate of teachers in areas where good facilities and stability of teaching personnel are most needed. The Newsom Report indicates forcefully that if we mean what we say about equality of educational opportunity this means unequal distribution of finance and resources to check the cumulative effect of social disadvantages.

This theme has been emphasized in a more recent report[9] on our Primary Schools, where special concern for children in what should be designated as 'Educational Priority Aims' is voiced. The report notes that 'some of these neighbourhoods have been starved of new schools, new houses and new investment of every kind'. Extra resources for schools in such areas

[8] *Half our Future* (The Newsom Report), London, H.M.S.O., 1963.
[9] *Children and their Primary Schools* (The Plowden Report), London, H.M.S.O., 1967.

are called for as a priority to compensate for poor homes and neighbourhoods. In the last few years big cities in America have mounted 'compensatory programmes' for children and adolescents who are clearly seen to be socially and therefore educationally deprived.

Allied to this interest in working-class children and their cultural deprivation, is a parallel resurgence of interest in the part environment plays in the stimulation of intelligence. The work of Hebb,[10] McV. Hunt[11] and others has led to a reappraisal of assumptions about the genetic foundation of intelligence in human development. Educators have written much more freely in the last decade about 'acquiring' intelligence. Despite dismal warnings that the quality of ability in the population is in decline, because those with the lowest intelligence tend to produce the most children, most surveys indicate that the general level of ability is rising. This may be due to increased affluence, better eating habits, the retreat of crippling poverty, the extension of the years of compulsory education, the stimulation of mass media and many other factors. Certainly, the phenomenal rise of numbers involved in higher education in both the U.S.A. and the U.S.S.R. seems to endorse the importance of the social stimulation of ability. In the Soviet Union alone, although the class structure is changing since the days of the revolution, vast numbers from the artisan and labouring classes avail themselves of opportunities for higher education through polytechnics, colleges and universities.

Yet in Britain there appears to be resistance to broadening the social intake of higher education, not only from those who favour continuing the education of an elite, but also from within the working-classes, particularly those more politically active and socially sensitive. They frequently express disquiet that to be better educated means to move into a middle-class way of life, with a consequent loss of working-class vitality and values. Is there some substance in this fear that working-class vitality, warmth, neighbourliness and loyalties will be destroyed by

[10] Hebb, D. O., *The Organisation of Behaviour*, New York, Wiley, 1949.

[11] Hunt, J. McV., *Intelligence and Experience*, New York, Ronald Press, 1961.

absorption into a different ethos, a more genteel and verbal culture? By greater equality of educational opportunity do we level *out* social inequalities, or do we level *up* and create a vast weighting of middle-class society with only a small rump of poorly educated working-class? While these questions are purely hypothetical, they form part of the dilemma of those involved in social mobility. It is interesting to read the following chapters with these questions in mind and to see how some of the contributors have determinedly retained their work-class identity but others have equally determinedly broken away from it.

Looking at all these questions afresh and viewing my own origins and subsequent education, it seemed to me that we have been hypnotized by the problems of social deprivation often to the exclusion of the potential that lies in the most apparently unpromising situation. This is not to minimize the extent of the problems of what we might call 'the socially disadvantaged', nor the importance of research into these matters. Yet it appears to me to be of great interest to see how, in the past, some individuals have found ways through the difficulties which impede them and have broken through into the open country of educational or vocational opportunity. The metaphor of breakthrough is somewhat limited, but it explains the title and purpose of this book.

The order in which I have arranged the chapters is alphabetical. Seven of the eleven contributors wrote their chapters, but four of them used a recorded interview with me (as a basis) which later was re-written into the final presentation. I wish to record my gratitude for their kindness, patience and particularly their frankness about their early years, without which this book would not have been possible.

RONALD GOLDMAN

I

JOHN ALLAWAY

*Vaughan Professor of Education, and Head of Department
of Adult Education, University of Leicester*

At the very end of the nineteenth century Sheffield's horse-drawn trams were replaced by electric vehicles and the tram-ways were extended in several directions co-incidentally with the outwards spread of the town. One direction they took was along Abbeydale Road towards Millhouses, then an area very largely in the country. About three miles from the town centre on the left of this main road and between it and the Midland Railway line, there was built a private estate, as it would now be called, of working-class houses; streets and streets of them, bearing names drawn from the Lake District; Windermere Road, Coniston Road, Buttermere Road. I was born on 5 June 1902 at No. 26 Rydal Road.

All the houses in 'Lakeland' were alike, two up and two down. Entrance to the parlour was direct from the street, and the kitchen opened on to a large asphalted yard. This was shared by four families, and at the rear of it stood two WCs, amenities not enjoyed by many working-class families. In both parlour and kitchen there was a cooking range and the kitchen also had a coal-fired wash-boiler. Bread-baking and washing on warm summer days was an ordeal, but a pleasant if infrequent experience was having a bath in a tub before a roaring fire on a winter's evening. The labour involved in heating the water was, however, prodigious.

My parents came as bride and groom to Rydal Road from Uxbridge, Middlesex, on the removal to Sheffield of my father's firm, in which he was a store-keeper, and I was born shortly after their arrival. My mother was the daughter of a gardener who had served under Florence Nightingale in the Crimea as a nursing orderly. She was twenty-eight and had been a cook in a Ladies' Academy. My paternal grandfather kept a public house—the Carpenters' Arms, Uxbridge—but before that he had spent twenty-one years as a constable in the Metropolitan Police Force. At the time of his marriage my father was twenty-six, and thought of himself as middle-class whereas my mother knew herself to be working-class. He was very tall and she quite diminutive.

Memories of life in Rydal Road are few. When I was about four years old we moved to 52 Aisthorpe Road, Woodseats. This too, formed part of a rapidly developing suburb, and consisted largely of working-class houses. Ours was new and of superior standard to the one we had left, but it lacked running hot water and a fixed bath, and it had no garden either back or front. The move suggests that my father's economic position had improved since, in addition to his having now to maintain my brother Jim as well as me, he felt able to pay more rent than hitherto. But it was a struggle on a wage of about twenty-seven shillings a week.

My father paid the rent and the coal bills and bought his own suits, and my mother fed and clothed us and paid the gas bills, and to enable her to do this she was given fifteen shillings a week. It was not always enough, especially after the birth of Mabel, my first sister, and towards the end of most weeks my mother would timidly ask for an extra shilling to do this or that. Her request was usually granted, but not without angry comments about wasteful spending. The taking out by my mother of industrial insurance policies at the rate of twopence a week on the lives of her three children particularly incensed my father, since he believed this kind of insurance a swindle on the public.

Our neighbours were all working people, but how different they were from each other! The Ealands belonged to the un-skilled working-class. Harry, the father, was a drayman, but he and his large family were easy-going folk who kept open house and were ever ready to help anyone in trouble. My father despised them for their untidyness and improvidence and was appalled by their familiarity. By contrast the Lemons belonged to the skilled working-class. Albert, the father, was a centre-lathe turner, with two daughters. They had a well-furnished and well-kept home, but were not very neighbourly. He was an active Trade-Unionist, Co-operator, Socialist and Atheist. To my father the Lemons were no more acceptable than the Ealands, for he detested everything they stood for.

My mother's relations with the Ealands and the Lemons were widely different. She was very friendly with Harry and Lizzie Ealand and with Mary Lemon. But of Albert Lemon she stood in awe, and not surprisingly, since he had no small talk, and when he spoke, which was rarely, it was with weighty seriousness. My father disapproved especially of my mother's association with the Ealands and complained that she was becoming like them, and I can well remember sharing his distress at this. I vividly recall feeling personally affronted when she took to wearing one of my father's old caps on going out to shop.

My school life began at four and a half years of age in the Woodseats Infant School and was continued at the Elementary School until I was twelve. But from the time I could read, much of my education took place in the outside WC. Here I avidly read *Thompson's Weekly*[1] and the *Family Journal*, contributed as toilet paper by the Ealands, and the *Daily Mail* and *Sheffield Telegraph* contributed by my family. My knowledge of current affairs became as ample as my admiration for Sir Edward Marshall Hall, who had the reputation of having saved more murderers from the hangman's noose than any other barrister. This clandestine reading was all the more pleasurable because in the house access to newspapers was strictly forbidden.

Around my tenth birthday the family moved again, this time to Cobnar Lodge, once the gatekeeper's house to a large mansion, but now on the edge of a series of workshops—a brass foundry, a manufactory of steel dolly-tubs and fireman's ladders—owned by Messrs Hattersley and Davidson, the firm

---

[1] This belonged to the same class of newspaper as the *News of the World*.

3

for which my father had worked since coming to Sheffield. He had recently been appointed Works Supervisor and the post carried with it a place to live. Cobnar Lodge, which was about a mile further out of town than the house we had left in Aisthorpe Road, had two rooms upstairs and three down and all were spacious. There was running hot and cold water and a fixed bath in the kitchen, and we had a large garden too.

By this time my father was already a far-gone consumptive. In running from Rydal Road to board a moving tram one winter's morning he had slipped and fallen heavily on his left elbow. The result was a diseased bone at the elbow which led the surgeons to advise amputation of the arm. The advice was rejected and, as a consequence, the elbow had to be poulticed daily for the remainder of his life. Gradually the infection spread throughout the body and, from time to time, my father had to spend months in sanitoria, which he found hateful, chiefly because he was a very active man and the régime imposed was one of inaction.

I loved wandering through the works, fascinated by the steel-pressing, galvanizing, brass-founding, acetylene-welding and blacksmithing being carried on, and also by the men's talk. Occasionally they would allow me to take over their jobs, and what a thrill it gave me to be engaged in *real* work. My greatest friend here was Walt, the resident engineer, by whom I was initiated into the mysteries of his trade and who won my heart by speaking to me as a fellow man. But, woe betide me if my father should find me feeding any of the machines or acting as blackmith's mate. 'Get out of here!' he would bark, 'And if I catch you at it again you'll feel the weight of my hand!'

At the time I did not realize that if an accident had occurred my father would have been held responsible. But he made no attempt to explain this to me. The resident engineer eventually did so. He and his wife Sal and their large family were our nearest neighbours. Unfeignedly working-class, they lived by the day and made little preparation for the future. In their untidy but warmly welcoming home I spent many happy hours. Walt was a staunch Trade-Unionist, Co-operator and Labour man. He read the *Daily News*,[2] which he allowed me to see, and he willingly answered any question I cared to ask him about what I was reading.

Rather oddly, it seemed to me, Walt's children, all of whom were older than I, followed no trade and were utterly indifferent to social and political questions. They took after their mother who was kindly but feckless. She spent many hours in our house gossiping and giving vivid descriptions of her various operations. My father detested her, and for Walt he had a mixture of envy and contempt, envy because of Walt's great skill as an engineer and his popularity with the workmen, and contempt for his apparent inability to make his will effective in his own home where everyone did much as he pleased.

As a Supervisor my father was feared and respected by the workmen. He cursed them when they were late or idle, but since he was the soul of punctuality and industry, they accepted his strictures with good grace. They knew that he expected of them no more than was fair and reasonable. But he was a boss's man and made no secret of it. He firmly believed that the worker ought to be grateful to his employer for his job and his wages and that he should express this gratitude by working hard and voting Conservative as his employer did. But he was hurt that they rejected his views and were distant and cool towards him.

My attitude towards my father was much the same as that of the workmen. I greatly respected him for his courage in the face of ill-health, his dogged determination, his firmness in dealing with most situations, and his loyalty to his employer. But I could not feel any great warmth or affection for him, whereas for my mother I had these feelings, but little respect. Whenever I had been beaten by my father and sent early to bed without food, I was contemptuous of my mother for creeping upstairs with soothing words and something for me to eat. This was to me a sign of weakness on her part. Why, I felt, could she not let me take my punishment like a man?

But I was bitter against my father for spending so much of

---

[2] A Lib-Lab paper which was subsequently taken over by the *Daily Chronicle* which became the *News Chronicle*.

his time and money at the Big Tree, a public house within a stone's throw of Cobnar Lodge. Here, by one means or another, he bought the personal popularity which was denied him at the works. Here he was the leading man, chairman of this club and that and Grand Master of the local Lodge of the Antediluvian Order of Buffaloes, the poor man's Masonic Order. I never saw my father drunk, but the knowledge that he spent more than he should have done on beer and cigarettes, and thus forced my mother to pinch and scrape more than she need have done to make ends meet, led to my becoming a determined teetotaller and non-smoker.

At the elementary school I did quite well, except in Standard IV, and in every standard occupied first to fourth place in classes of about sixty pupils. In Standard IV we had a teacher who must have believed that fear is the beginning of wisdom, since he freely used a broad thick leather strap on all who failed to measure up to his expectations of them. Falling short of these in mathematics on one occasion I was severely beaten, with disastrous results. So I was beaten again and again. This teacher was killed in action during the early part of the First World War, and I can remember when I heard this saying to myself, 'I'm glad, I'm glad,' but at the same time feeling very, very guilty.

Although my attendance record at school was excellent, since nothing would keep me away except infectious illness, and although my place in the class was always at or near the top, I never won a prize of any kind. This I attributed to prejudice on the part of my teachers. Whether this was fantasy or reality I know not, but I believed that they consistently overlooked my claims to recognition because I was small, poorly dressed and was working-class in speech. It seemed to me that our teachers showed a preference for, and gave more time and attention to, pupils belonging to their own class. However, since my scholastic achievement was good, I found school life, on the whole, satisfying.

When the time came for choosing pupils to be groomed for the secondary-school examinations my class marks were too good to be ignored. I could have become a member of that select group which occupied the centre of Standard V classroom and received the teacher's special attention, but my father said 'No.' He told the Headmaster that he did not believe in children and young people being educated beyond their station, and that an elementary education was all that I required. But, even if he had believed otherwise, my father could not then have afforded the cost of a grammar-school education for me. I knew this and was not too disappointed, but I silently vowed that somehow I would get myself a higher education.

Although he never set foot in any church, except for a wedding or a funeral, my father was a firm believer in religion, especially for the young. So we children were sent to Sunday School at an early age, first to the nearby 'Bloody Ranters' Tin Chapel,' as my father called the Primitive Methodist School, and later, when we had settled in Cobnar Lodge, to Mr. Cammell's Schoolroom. This edifice, built as an act of piety by one of the Directors of Messrs. Cammell Laird, the great steel and shipbuilding firm, was in effect an Anglican mission church, anti-Roman Catholic and anti-Anglo-Catholic, fundamentalist and with a taste for British Israelism.

By the time I was twelve years old scouting had great attractions for me but, alas, I could not afford a uniform, and thus could not join an established troop. Not to be baulked, however, I persuaded seven other boys in a like financial plight to my own to form a patrol and Tom Morton, Superintendent of Cammell's Sunday School, to become our Scoutmaster, my rôle being that of Patrol Leader. We bought various items of uniform as we could, and by acting for some months as lather boy to a barber on every evening of the week except scout night, I was able to find the money to equip myself tolerably well. When all were uniformed we joined the Northern Church Troop as an additional patrol.

Those of us not destined to move on to a secondary school were now transferred to Abbeydale Higher Elementary School, three miles distant from home. We greatly enjoyed the walk except in bad weather. Here we were assigned to Standard VII in a school which made appreciably higher demands on our intellectual powers than the one we had left. It was housed in an old and ill-equipped building, and because it lacked suitable text-books we were expected to buy our own. This almost led to my being withdrawn and sent elsewhere, since my father firmly believed it to be the L.E.A.'s duty to provide a really *free* education.

However, I was not withdrawn, but being without text-books would have placed me at a serious disadvantage had not my desk companion, Eric Church, been willing to share his with me both in school and in his home, where we did our homework together. There was a lot to do but I said nothing about it in my own home, since my father was strenuously opposed to any kind of homework. We responded well to the challenge of the new school and soon were promoted to Standard VIII, which contained only about twenty boys. Here we came under the influence of Tommy Cross, a very remarkable teacher who made learning an exciting adventure and, for me at least, opened new windows on the world.

The first thing we noticed on joining the class was a frequent breaching of the time-table. There it was on the wall, showing that the first hour was for Scripture, the second for Arithmetic, the third for English and so on. But we found Scripture this day taking up all morning, and mathematics all afternoon, and on other days History, Geography and English all being taught together. Although I never heard him mention the unity of knowledge, Tommy Cross vividly brought it home to us in his classroom teaching. But he also set us to work a great deal singly and in twos and threes, and as we worked he moved round among us asking questions and giving advice and encouragement.

Tommy Cross introduced us to Mark Twain's *Huckleberry Finn* and *Tom Sawyer*, Harrison Ainsworth's *Jack Sheppard*, Gustave Doré's *The Adventures of Baron Munchausen*, Felix Gras' *The Reds of the Midi* and Jack London's *Wild Fang* and *The Call of the Wild*, for their own sake and as models to follow in creative writing, which he set us to do. Gathered round him we would listen to readings from these books and discuss key passages. Once in an Art session he dumped an old boot on my desk and said, 'Make a pen and ink sketch of this.' It seemed an odd request, since the only Art I had previously done in school consisted in copying pictures from instructional cards published by Messrs. E. J. Arnold, the educational furnishers. I count it one of the greatest privileges of my life to have been a pupil of this superb teacher.

Before coming under the influence of Tommy Cross I had become an omnivorous reader. Newspapers, which I now openly read at home, magazines and books of all kinds were grist to my mill. I read so much that my parents, neither of whom ever looked into a book, really believed that so much reading would turn my brain. But Tommy Cross caused me to be more selective in what I read and I began to limit myself to books on scientific discovery, engineering wonders, adventure and crime detection. The novels of George Alfred Henty held me spellbound, *Robinson Crusoe* and *The Swiss Family Robinson* I found absorbing, and I became a fervent admirer of Mr. Sherlock Holmes.

The First World War broke out whilst I was still at school and for two years the backward and forward movement of the battle lines in France were followed with great interest in the classroom where they were shown on a large wall-map. But by 1916 I found myself playing a minor rôle in the European struggle as an engineer's apprentice in the down-town works of my father's firm, for there all of us were most of the time engaged on war-work, and particularly on the manufacture of trench-mortars. My working week was one of fifty-four hours, and for it, as an indentured apprentice, I received the sum of five shillings which would rise by varying annual increments to sixteen shillings in my twenty-first year.

I had not been at work more than a month before my father died, at the age of thirty-nine, leaving my mother with three of us to maintain—my younger sister Winifred, born in 1914 and now two years of age, my sister Mabel, ten years of age, my brother Jim, twelve years of age, and myself. My mother had the widow's pension of ten shillings a week and my wages, which together were insufficient to cover our needs, especially as the price of everything was mounting. We, therefore, took in a young man and his wife as lodgers, and my mother found part-time work as a cleaner. Later she also became a part-time canteen worker in the Cobnar Lodge works because, on being moved to a small house on the works estate, a 'two up and two down' with no amenities, we had to send our lodgers away.

Although the firm I worked for made no systematic arrangements (as was promised in the indentures) to train its apprentices, I made good progress in learning my trade, thanks to help received from some of the older hands. In the evenings I attended the Woodseats 'Night School' and completed the three years' course in Mathematics, Mechanics, Machine-drawing and English, gaining a first-class in every subject. This entitled me to a place at the Central Evening School, but I could not accept it, since the family was unable to afford even the nominal fees charged, or the cost of instruments and books. Thus I found another avenue to higher education closed to me.

The most significant influences in my life between the ages of fourteen and seventeen were those of the Norton Church Scout Troop and Cammell's School. In the Troop I successfully became Senior Patrol Leader and Acting Assistant Scoutmaster and, in the absence on war service of the officers, in effect its Scoutmaster. At Cammell's School I found myself from time to time conducting the children's Morning Service and regularly teaching in the afternoon school. Here I was given the fullest encouragement and support by Tom Morton, who treated me as though I were his son. Through these experiences I developed a confidence in inter-personal relations which had been lacking in me as a schoolboy.

When I was just turned eighteen my mother died at the age of forty-four of a kidney disease. Poverty, overwork, anxiety and lack of proper medical attention had undoubtedly hastened her end. I had the task, since there were no near relations who could help, of attending to the funeral, and arranging for the care of my brother and sisters. My brother, who was then a joiner's apprentice, went to live with the Ealands, and later became a soldier, and my sisters were placed in one of the cottage homes of the Ecclesall Poor Law Guardians. Another task which fell to my lot was the selling up of our home. Few of the buyers showed any generosity and the total receipts came to less than thirty pounds, which I banked on behalf of the four of us. I went into lodgings with friends.

About this time I came into contact with the Seventh Day Adventists and but for their fantastic interpretations of prophecy I might have become one of them. For I saw that if, as my Cammell's School friends believed, the Bible interpreted literally is to be taken as the sole basis of faith, there is no scriptural warrant whatever for Sunday Observance. But what led me to part with the Adventists and ultimately with the School, was my reading half a dozen issues of a short-lived Popular Science monthly named, as far as I can recall, *Conquest*, which resulted in my conversion to Evolutionism and, through the 'Higher Criticism' as it was then called, to my looking at the Bible with entirely fresh eyes.

I had now become a lay preacher, occupying the pulpit once a month in our Schoolroom, and pulpits in other mission churches occasionally. As my addresses began to be influenced by the new knowledge which *Conquest* had stimulated me to acquire, Tom Morton and his fellows became rather worried. What kind of bird had they hatched in Mr. Cammell's nest? But they did not more than patiently question, and express dissent from my developing ideas. In addition to these opportunities for self-expression, however, Cammell's School gave me others, particularly through membership of its Mutual Improvement Society which met weekly during the winter months round a roaring open wood fire.

Through listening to papers on all kinds of topics—religious, historical, literary, geographical and political—and the subsequent discussions, through preparing and reading papers myself, and through the editorship of the Society's newspaper, I learned a great deal. But I also found myself growing out of sympathy with the leading members, my beloved Tom Morton among them. They were politically Conservative, anti-Trade-Union and anti-co-operative in their outlook, whereas I was becoming the very opposite. But about this, too, they were understanding, and when the break came with both the Society and the School, it was through my own doing, and the parting was a sorrowful one on both sides.

During the years from sixteen to twenty-one much of my life, other than that spent at the works, was largely centred on Cammell's School. Here I found scope for the expression of a developing personality, in conducting services, preaching, lecturing and discoursing with older friends on a great variety of topics, and here, too, I found pleasure in the company of its members. At the Soirées of the Mutual Improvement Society and the School's social gatherings we would sing rather sentimental ballads round the piano, hear each other perform his party piece and stage a one-act play from the long list of farces published by Messrs. Abel Heywood of Manchester. Our cultural sights were not set very high, but we enjoyed what we did together.

Through Tom Morton, who was manager of the scythe and sickle Department at Messrs. W. Tyzack, Sons and Turner, I was introduced to homes and a way of life far more gracious than I had known as a boy. There were, for example, Tom's own home, presided over with unaffected charm by his wife, Jane; the home of his married niece, Hilda Rowland, where I lodged happily for several years, and the home of Joe Johnson, a scrivener, who was also an Assistant Registrar of Births, Deaths and Marriages. From him I learned to write a beautiful hand but, alas, taking down lecture notes as an undergraduate later, irremediably ruined it.

At work I became a reasonably competent journeyman-fitter at a gross wage of three pounds for a forty-eight hour week, which I rarely earned, owing to short-time working. I was now an active member of the Amalgamated Engineering Union, first as Doorkeeper[3] of the Sheffield No. 2 Branch and later as its Assistant Secretary and representative on the Trades and Labour Council. As a keen Labour man I was a regular reader of the *Daily Herald*, then under the editorship of George Lansbury, and the *New Leader*, brilliantly edited by H. N. Brailsford, ably supported by the economists J. A. Hobson and E. F. Wise, and by the humorist 'Yaffle' whose identity I have never discovered.

The times were, however, very bad. There were weeks when my earnings came to less than the twenty-five shillings I was paying for board and lodging and I began to fear that I should have to move to poor working-class accommodation. On seeing my plight Tom Morton promised me a regular job as a scythe

[3] A position which had survived from the days when Trade-Unions were secret societies. Its main function had become that of collecting the 'pence cards' and dues from members' wives and children who sat in a passageway to the Branch Meeting Room.

fitter and the prospect of piece-work earnings well above three pounds a week. But when I came to ask him to redeem his promise he gave only evasive replies. At this I felt heavily let down, since there was no man I trusted more than he. And when a few months later he found a similar job for his niece's husband my faith in human nature was utterly confounded.

In my early twenties I came across Frederick Winslow Taylor's *Principles of Scientific Management*, and was led by it to read widely in the subject. I began at once to apply to my own work Time and Motion Study and other means of speeding up production. As soon as the firm's management saw what I was up to it made me a kind of acting Production Engineer (unpaid). My fellow workers were puzzled. Was I a boss's man after all? I tried to persuade them that their 'go slow' policy was a mistaken one and could only land them at the door of the Labour Exchange, but my efforts were fruitless. They were tolerant of their wayward young colleague, however, and this enabled us to remain on good terms.

One evening in 1925 at a choir meeting in Cammell's School, a woman member passed round copies of a handbill which invited its readers to attend a lecture arranged by the Workers' Educational Association. It was to be given by a Mr. H. L. Beales, M.A., of Sheffield University, and would deal with 'The Gold Standard.' I had not previously heard of the W.E.A., but at once I knew, without a shadow of doubt, that this was *the* thing for me. And so it proved. The lecture was in the nature of bait to attract students to a three years' Tutorial Class in Local Government, with Beales as the tutor, and I swallowed the bait whole. At the first meeting I was made Class Secretary and before long I found myself a member of the Executive Committee of the Sheffield Branch of the Association.

Through membership of Beales's class I made my first contact with the world of scholarship, and what an adventurous experience it was. Beales is a first-rate teacher (happily he is still with us) who can share easily and with all kinds of men his great wealth of knowledge, especially of English Social History in the early period of England's industrialization. His humanity and urbanity, as well as his scholarship, captured my heart at once. As well as an eager listener to his lectures and an active participant in class discussion, I became an avid reader of the books he recommended and an industrious essay writer. The year I spent under him was full of inspiration.[4] At the end of it Beales urged me to apply for an Oxford Adult Scholarship, although normally applications were considered only from those who had completed their studies in a Tutorial Class. I did so and was summoned for interview, but failed to obtain a place. I was, however, encouraged to try again next year, which I decided to do. Meanwhile, I joined the first year of another Tutorial Class, one in Psychology taken by Geoffrey Thompson, also of the University of Sheffield. Although not in the same class as Beales as scholar or teacher, Thompson was a competent tutor, and under his guidance I learned much. At the end of my second year in the W.E.A. I tried to get into Oxford again, and once more was unsuccessful.

By now I was married to a girl I had known for about seven years. She was the daughter of a bricklayer, and I had met her at my place of work. I was also by now a Unitarian and she and I regularly worshipped at Upper Chapel; we were indeed married there. It had an upper-middle-class congregation at its morning services and at its evening services an upper-working-to lower-middle-class congregation. We belonged to the latter. Upper Chapel then had as its minister the Rev. Alfred Hall, a man of wide learning and liberal views. He seemed to take to me at once and in friendship with him, his delightful family and their circle, I found much pleasure and profit.

I was now in my twenty-sixth year. My work was interesting and it looked promising. Surely one day I might become a real Production Engineer! I was happy in serving the A.E.U. and at being thought of as a likely full-time Trade-Union official or a Labour M.P. The friendships I had made at Upper Chapel and the prospects which were opening up of active participation in chapel affairs I found very satisfying. And the rewards of study in W.E.A. classes and in working for the W.E.A. were immense. All these reconciled me to what seemed to be my fate, that is, never to achieve my youthful ambition to obtain

---

[4] He left Sheffield shortly afterwards for the London School of Economics where he became Reader in Economic History. He is now retired but still very active.

a formal higher education. I had seen the grammar-school closed against me, the technical high-school and Oxford, but I was not at all discontented.

Then one evening in June 1928 after I had gone to bed, two callers—Alan McPhee,[5] tutor in the third year of the W.E.A. class in Local Government, and another—asked to see me. I hastily rose and was informed that they had come straight from a meeting of the Sheffield University Joint Committee for Tutorial Classes to invite me forthwith to apply for a Sir Ernest Cassel Scholarship tenable at the University. I thanked them, but at first refused because the scholarship was for one year only and I could not afford, with trade being so bad, to give up my job for a course which might lead nowhere. On their assuring me, however, that the Committee had thought of that and was prepared to guarantee me financial support for three years I gave them the answer they sought.

Next day the application form was completed and despatched and shortly afterwards I was informed that I had been awarded the Scholarship. Now, having the necessary funds behind me for one year at least, I had to gain entry into the University. Fortunately its Ordinances made special provision for 'persons of mature age' which at twenty-six I was considered to be, and under this provision a special matriculation examination, tailored to my circumstances, was set. This I passed. At the end of the third week in September I handed in to Hattersley and Davidson Ltd. my notice to leave, and quickly passed from being a journeyman-fitter to an undergraduate reading for Honours in Economics.

Although there were four other adult students reading economics, these were exceptions. In other departments there was none. Overwhelmingly the undergraduates were from eighteen to twenty-one years of age and, although only five years separated me from the eldest of them, it seemd to these and to me as though it might have been three or four times as much. Experience of life, and especially of industrial life, placed a great gulf between us which we found difficult to

[5] At that time a Staff Tutor for Tutorial Classes in Sheffield and subsequently Director of Extra-mural Studies, first in Liverpool and later in London.

bridge. As a consequence the few adult students in the university came to form a separate and closely-knit group. We came also to join more or less the same student societies and, unfortunately, to dominate them. It seemed to me that if universities are to admit adult students, they should do so far more widely than was then the case.

My first experiences of university teaching were disappointing. I had been used to the informal learning situations provided by the Mutual Improvement Society and the W.E.A. class, with the ample opportunities they provided for questions and discussion, and I was amazed at the formality of the university lecture system, the aloofness of the university teacher from his students, the perfunctoriness of much of the teaching and the evident reluctance of many university teachers to answer questions or to allow themselves to be drawn into discussion. Within the Department of Economics, under the headship of Professor Douglas Knoop, things were rather better, but in most other Departments they were bad, not only for Pass-Degree students, who were nobody's business, but for Honours students also.

Towards the end of my first year, although I had consistently obtained very good marks for essay work and in terminal examinations, I felt disheartened with life at the university, and especially with the university as an educational device. It seemed to me so lacking both in efficiency and humanity. However, in spite of this, I determined to stick it out and, although I never ceased to feel that what *was* fell woefully short of what *might be* and *ought to be*, I gradually accommodated myself to the régime and made steady progress as a student. As I passed on to the second and third years, the learning situation within the Economics Department became more friendly and informal but, from conversations with fellow undergraduates, I gathered that in most departments this did not happen.

Professor Knoop was a bachelor, and his mother, a charming old lady of German origin, kept house for him. Mrs. Knoop took her rôle as the Professor's lady very seriously, keeping an eagle eye on the doings of the wives of younger members of the staff and discreetly instructing them in their social duties. She also entertained all the Honours students in Economics to afternoon tea once a term. It was for most of us an education in itself, since we had never previously been involved in this middle-middle to upper-middle class custom. I cannot pretend that any of us found it a comfortable learning situation. Mother and son did their best to draw us out and to get conversation going, but they were never really successful. Every student breathed a sigh of relief when, at a few minutes to six, it was all over. And, I dare say, Knoop and his mother did the same when all of us had gone.

In the earlier years of my course the economics teaching was based on the works of Alfred Marshall, of whom Knoop was a faithful disciple. I found Marshall uncongenial. His marginal theory and his theory of distribution (which was bound up with his marginalism) I viewed with deep suspicion. What I was interested in was not how the rent of land per acre, the rate of interest and hourly wage-rates were determined, but why some men (some of whom did no work at all) were rich and others poor, and how this situation could be altered without diminishing the source of all incomes. So, I read well outside the limits of the set books—works by J. A. Hobson, Edwin Cannan, Henry George, Gustav Cassell, Hugh Dalton and John Maynard Keynes—and incorporated the fruits of my reading in essays and examination scripts.

Yet, although I read widely, took part in a number of university student activities and continued to pursue my pre-university interests, I never felt heavily pressed for time. Around me I saw students who seemed to work far harder at their studies than I, but whose academic achievements were not as good, so that at times I suffered from strong feelings of guilt. Somehow I seemed to be getting rewards beyond my deserts. So three years went by. At the end of it I obtained an excellent degree and the Gladstone Prize in Economics, and was offered the Town Trust Fellowship for two years. But that was in 1931, the year of the Great Depression. The chance came my way of a job as a Manchester University Resident Tutor for extra-mural studies in Rossendale, Lancashire, and was too good a thing to miss. I took it and declined the Fellowship.

Looking back over the years up to the time of graduation, I am impressed by the extent which luck played in my life.

I was lucky in early childhood to have developed the need-disposition to prove myself against my father, and in having a father who was so conservative in his outlook. This need-disposition carried me forward, in spite of many difficulties and disappointments. But I was also lucky in coming under the influence of two truly great teachers—Tommy Cross and H. L. Beales—and in my connections with Cammell's Schoolroom. Nevertheless, I do believe that educational opportunity should not rest on chance in so far as the community can prevent its doing so.

II

DEREK DAVIES

Headmaster, Minehead School

The Black Country where I was born and grew up was the creation of the Industrial Revolution, and it is hard to think of any area of England which better typifies the results of that careless, greedy rape. Welsh pits, Lancashire cotton mills, Tyneside shipyards have produced their grim working-conditions and their grimmer living-conditions, but nothing, I think, quite equals the berserk ravaging of the land which went on in the area to the immediate north of Birmingham. Even today the sprawling conurbation spilling out from Birmingham towards West Bromwich, Walsall and Wolverhampton bears the scars and is a planner's nightmare. To a Victorian guide-book writer it looked like this:

The whole district round about here is a mass of apparent disorganisation, confusion and ruin. By day we see nothing but the remains of the disembowelling of the earth; heaps of stones, clay, coal, cinders and ashes, as if a volcano had burst out and covered the country with its lava; furnaces, chimneys, forges and iron works, beds of burning coal, coal pits with their engines and apparatus, and waggons conveying loads of stone and coal in every direction. . . . The whole is constantly enveloped in the gloom of one perpetual cloud of smoke, which bedims and darkens the country for miles around.

By night the country around is lit up by fires. . . . From a hill near this town, toward Sedgley, at night, nearly two hundred blast furnaces, for the smelting of iron from the ore, may be seen; a sight which cannot be had, probably, in any other part of the world.[1]

[1] *Osborne's Guide to the Grand Junction, or Birmingham, Liverpool and Manchester Railway, with the Topography of the country through which the Line passes.* E. C. & W. Osborne, 30 Bennett's Hill, Birmingham, 1838, p. 139.

When I was in the Sixth Form at Wolverhampton Grammar-School I came across the book from which that passage is taken in a local second-hand bookshop and did a piece on it for the school magazine. It was a funny piece since it was easy to poke fun at Victorian pomposity, and score points off the archaic exaggeration. Yet looking back now from middle-age and with some historical reading behind me, I am not so sure that the basic differences between 1838 and 1938 were so great. Certainly in the last twenty years the Black Country has been altered almost out of recognition. For one thing some of the most obvious factors which made it black—literally black: black to the eye and black to the touch, layer upon layer of encrusted industrial dirt—have disappeared. Such coal-working as remains has been concentrated in a few large scientifically-managed pits. The multitude of small blast-furnaces have either gone out of business or been swallowed up in the growing amalgamations of the steel industry. And the energetic but filthy child of the marriage of coal and iron, the steam-engine, is rapidly becoming a thing of the past. The Black Country is infinitely cleaner.

Many of the 'heaps of stones, clay, coal, cinders and ashes' have been levelled and landscaped to provide sites for ever-spreading housing estates, and however unsightly those may be in their own way, they offer a tamed and tidy aspect compared with what was there before. Industry has increased throughout the area, but most of it is light industry and follows the pattern of 'industrial estate' development which can be found almost anywhere in England. Similarly major road developments have imposed a pattern which could be found almost anywhere in the country in the vicinity of large towns.

However, in 1923 when I was born, I think the guide-book writer would still have recognized his landscape as substantially the same. He was looking from Bilston straight across my birthplace, Coseley, for three or four miles to the edge of the Black Country. The 'hill toward Sedgley' I knew as 'the Beacon', the one high point on my childhood horizon. From it one could look to the West to deep, green countryside stretching to the Severn and beyond where it was always possible for an active lad with a bicycle to get away blackberrying or bird-nesting or fishing within a matter of twenty minutes at most. But with one's back to the green one's eye could run in an unbroken arc from Wolverhampton's urban mass to the North, through Bilston straight ahead, and on for another twelve miles or more of smoke and haze stretching to 'Brummagem'. The night-sky was still made red by the furnaces, and for the first sixteen years of my life the thump and roar of their blast was as natural a part of my existence as my own heartbeat. The only item omitted from the guide's description was the traces of the land's original purely agricultural condition, odd, tiny pockets of farmland eking out an anomalous existence in this morass of industrial squalor.

Martin Street, the street in which I lived from the age of two, ran for a mere thirty houses off the main Parkfield Road where I was born. An extra half-dozen council houses had been added at a much later date. The street surface was not made up until I was seven, and in winter it was a mass of pot-holes and puddles. Beyond the council houses it continued as a rough dirt track leading to a large scrap-yard. Between each pair of terraced houses there ran a brick tunnel or 'entry'. Originally such tunnels had given access to a small yard, beyond which was a separate wash-house and an old-style closet, which had to be emptied periodically. There was a significant class-distinction between those families who left their entry open and those, like us, who covered in the yard area with a home-made wooden structure dignified by the name of 'verandah', and added a high wooden door to it to secure a degree of privacy. These additions turned the entries into dark, echoing places suitable for various acts of childish vandalism, such as knocking loudly on the door in the appropriate season and decamping rapidly when somebody came to open it, leaving a lighted 'banger' to explode.

Because the street stuck out from a main road, casually introduced with no eye to subsequent development, a narrow peninsula of houses projecting into the surrounding sea of wasteland, there was no back-to-back building, and this saved it handsomely from being a slum. The builder who had run up the houses even provided token gardens at the back, and most of the families cultivated these intensively for vegetables. Many also had sheds at the bottom of the garden in which they kept poultry as a further supplement to the family budget. The solid brick wall which bounded each garden had holes knocked into it wherever necessary, and the hens ranged freely out to the pickings they could find on the derelict land beyond.

This land was my childish kingdom, and rejoiced in the local name of The Black Piles. This description had no repulsion for me since it was not until late adolescence that I met the word piles in a medical context. For me it was as matter-of-fact as my own name, and it was literally precise. For the best part of a square mile between the house and the nearest furnaces there were piles of coal-dust and pit spoil, dumped higgledy-piggledy, wherever fancy had taken. On the edges of the area sturdy coarse grass grew, but the predominant impression was of a black lunar landscape. Here and there were craggy mounds of slag, the lava-like skimmings from molten iron-ore, jettisoned by the furnace-men in the same careless manner, and in one or two places the local refuse lorries tipped their household rubbish. Both our poultry and my playmates found rich pickings on these 'tips'.

To complete the vision of chaos a second 'disembowelling of the earth' was taking place. The slag heaps provided ideal material for road-making, and so to long-established local firms such as Hickmans (later to become part of the Stewarts and Lloyds combine), and John Thompson Boilers and Tubes, there was added Tarmac Ltd. Lorry-load after lorry-load of slag was dug out and carted away to be crushed and treated to produce improved road surfaces. Hence The Black Piles became a labyrinth of lorry tracks, winding between the man-made hills of coal dust and ending in cliff-faces of slag. I do not think I have ever found any adult experience to rival the satisfaction I had as a child—spiced by the danger of being caught by the 'ganger' of the site or even an occasional policeman patrolling the workings—of hurling a carefully chosen piece of slag at a strategic point in the face to bring crashing down eight or ten tons of the stuff at one go!

Nowadays when I read accounts of children's 'Adventure playgrounds' or study ways of keeping my own younger pupils happily occupied, my thoughts run back to The Black Piles.

DEREK DAVIES

If only one could reproduce their facilities, with some reduction of the grosser dangers, one could create a remarkably challenging and satisfying playground. Practically any standard children's game fitted in well, and some gained tremendously from the natural hazards of the terrain. Cowboys and Indians was a much more realistic affair with real hills and valleys in miniature to gallop over, and winding stage-coach trails (thoughtfully provided by the slag lorries) for ambushes. For my money no version of Hide and Seek will ever match our variant of Kick the Can. The recipe was: obtain one fair-sized tin-can from the tip, place it on the edge of a slag cliff, get the strongest boy of the group to kick it hard over the brink, and scatter to hide while the one that is 'on' scrambles wildly down and back up again over the treacherous, rocky, shifting surface. Provided one did not object to the colour, the ridges of coal dust were virtually interchangeable with sand-dunes, and dusky figures in swimming trunks slid noisily down many a chute. In my mind's eye every child from those days looks at me out of dust-rimmed eyes, like so many diminutive miners coming off shift.

The really idiosyncratic games grew directly out of the traditions that had produced the terrain. For a century and a half men had dug 'gin-pits' there, small two- or three-man enterprises, or often man-wife ventures, he to dig and she to haul up the bucket. Therefore we dug pits. We rarely got more than ten or twelve feet down before the sheer hard labour damped our enthusiasm, but as coal could be found almost anywhere in this ground within inches of the surface, we got all we wanted. Coal was obviously there to be burned, and so we built fires, much more for the sheer pleasure of getting them going, of producing smoke and heat and flames, than to cook on them, although cooking was done, Chimney fashions were elaborate. Old bricks lay about by the hundred, and clay abounded at certain spots. Brick upon brick could be bonded together with clay which rapidly hardened in the fire's heat, and the chimneys reached precarious heights, to be surmounted by an old bucket with its bottom knocked out as a final gesture. Portable fire-cans were also very popular. An old tin-can with nail-holes knocked in to afford draught could be slung on a loop of wire

23

the length of one's arm, and when filled with glowing coals and swung round and round the head in complicated patterns made a fine sight at night, and a positively diabolical weapon.

All these resources and skills came to bear on our most characteristic occupation, building a 'hovel'. This word, too, had no literary connotations until I was well into Grammar-School, and when I met it in its normal context I had to make a conscious mental adjustment. For me a hovel meant half a dozen boys planning and working together to excavate an oblong hole perhaps eight feet by twelve and at least six feet deep, to be roofed over and camouflaged with a thick layer of spoil. The materials for the roof, beams of wood or metal rods followed by old doors or corrugated-iron sheets, were readily available from the scrapyard if one did not mind barbed-wire fences, 'Keep Out' notices, and ultimately the Police Court. A flight of steps would be dug for the entrance, heating and cooking would be provided for by taking underground one of our fireplaces, and any number of elaborations could be added as the long summer holidays went on such as seats, food-stores, and lighting. Sometimes these structures survived from one summer to the next, but more often as they served as gang headquarters they succumbed to rival gang attacks and were left wrecked and abandoned at the end of the holidays. Despite their similarity to First World War dug-outs I can remember no suggestion at all that we were imitating what our fathers must have done only a decade before in the trenches. We found our models in similar shelters scattered about the area by the men who for longer decades had worked the mineral wealth of the region. Fundamentally our hovels provided what 'dens' have provided for children in many ages—a base independent of home where, within certain limits, we could lead unfettered lives and pursue our fantasies wherever they led.

My parents disapproved of the hovels, and I was never allowed to live and sleep in one for days or even weeks at a time as some of the children did. My parents disapproved of many things about The Black Piles and our environment generally. They aspired to better things, if not for themselves then for their only child, who seemed to be bright and ought to win a 'scholarship' to the Grammar-School. They said the hovels were dangerous and somebody would be buried alive one day. This was palpable nonsense, for they were surprisingly stoutly built, but I did not argue since I recognized intuitively that the dangers they meant were of a different kind and a kind not to be discussed in our house. The least danger was learning to smoke, and this I avoided easily enough until, ironically, I reached the summit of my ambitions and became an Oxford scholar. Whereas other students swore by black coffee to help produce essays late at night, I found coffee totally indigestible and turned for aid to cigarettes. The real danger and the truly unmentionable one was sex. And this temptation I did succumb to. The hovels were predominantly male affairs, but a certain number of girls hovered on the fringe and on occasion were pulled—often literally—into the male club. Since the age limit for hovel society was fourteen, when the children left school, took a job and had virtually no free time, and since we were all a good deal less sophisticated about sex than children seem to be today, nothing very dramatic happened. A fair amount of exploratory fumbling went on between both boys and girls and boys and boys, and we all added a little to our meagre stock of sexual knowledge and more extensive stock of dirty stories. Possibly more happened than I ever knew, for I did not last to the fourteen age-limit. I won my scholarship and the old close ties with the other children of the street steadily weakened. I was told by my parents that The Black Piles were not for me, and within a year or two I came to accept the decision. I became an alien in my own environment.

On the face of it we were working-class, but we were much more willing to accept that label for our neighbours than for ourselves. Both my maternal grandparents were Black Country workers to the core. My grandmother, Ruth Perry, was born at Cradley Heath, and until her marriage worked in a little home forge in the back yard making nails by hand. My grandfather, Joseph Parkes, was the son of a Tipton innkeeper whose establishment gained some fame as the haunt of 'The Tipton Slasher', a noted bare-fisted pugilist. He himself was a good athlete in his youth and a hard drinker later in life, common enough characteristics amongst the men who did the hot, mauling work of rollers in Hickman's rolling mill. On my father's side there may have been a touch of something different. According to family tradition my great-grandmother came of 'a good family' and married beneath her. Whether the alleged come-down was due to her marrying an insurance agent, or to the reputation she had for being the spitting image of Queen Victoria, I have never discovered. Certainly her daughter, Mary Hardy, did nothing to restore lost status, for she married Joseph Jacob Davies, who spent most of his working life as a fitter in various Black Country engineering works, and had a jovial philosophy of life which almost amounted to fecklessness. He was the only grandparent alive during my childhood, and for some years he lived in our house. He was then doing unskilled heavy labouring well beyond his strength and years, but he still frequently proclaimed his basic philosophy in broad Black Country dialect—'If 'ee doh cum, 'ee sends'. This could be held to apply to the Almighty, I think, but certainly to better-off friends who might occasionally help out. Eventually he was fully justified in his faith. At the age of seventy-two he married a woman of considerable property in Bilston, and lived his last days with his every want supplied. If he had Welsh blood in him, as the surname Davies suggests, it originated further back than his parents, who were solidly English and came from Kidderminster.

My mother, baptized Leah Ann but always known as Daisy, left school at twelve and served her time as a tailoress with Southan Brothers in Wolverhampton. My father, Benjamin (how the Biblical names recur in this area where Methodism held sway), won the chance of a place at the Wolverhampton Higher Grade School, but preferred to leave at the minimum age to start as an apprentice in a rolling-mill. Had this job continued he might have done very well, perhaps becoming a foreman or even a manager, for the steel industry still recruited its managers from the mill floor. But he volunteered early in the First World War and was badly wounded shortly before the Armistice, losing two fingers and narrowly avoiding having a leg amputated. This ruled out the heavy work of the rolling-mill, and whatever his original scope might have been he now had to start at the bottom once more, learning a new

trade as a die-caster at the Sunbeam motor works in Wolverhampton. When I was seven the 1930 slump ended Sunbeam's
career as an independent firm, and after a period of unemployment he had to make yet another start. This time he was glad
to be taken on as a labourer with a small firm which made
rollers for processing all kinds of metal.

Despite these setbacks I grew up in an aura of vague hope and
aspiration. My father's uncle had risen in a steel works to
become a manager, but he had migrated to John Summers'
steelworks near Chester in the process, and was a tantalizingly
distant figure who appeared very occasionally with impressive
signs of affluence. There was a car (a truly significant status
symbol in the early 1930s), photographs of seaside holidays at
his own caravan, and dazzling Christmas presents which must
have cost at least five shillings. My father's brother had also
made his way in industry with considerable success, but he, too,
had left the dictrict and was equally remote. It never seriously
crossed my mind that I should emulate these relatives. Had
they been nearer at hand my ambition might have been fired
towards industry, but what I saw of industry repelled me. Sometimes when my father worked overtime at weekends, doing
maintenance jobs to add to his pay-packet, I would take him
a can of tea and a midday meal in a tin basin, and the deserted,
dark and dirty machine-shop where I found him had no attractions for me. What these distant success stories did foster in
me was a conviction that somehow, despite our straitened
circumstances, we were still distinctly a cut above the *real*
working class who lived next door.

Other factors nourished this belief. My mother had been
brought up as a Primitive Methodist and was an active and
respected member of the Chapel community. Through her I
had some standing in the Chapel, although I found it increasingly difficult to accept in my adolescence the Chapel's form of
service, with long extempore prayers from visiting lay-
preachers, and even longer sermons. She was a house-proud
woman and an excellent manager of our slim budget. By using
her skill as a tailoress to make many of our clothes, and by
bottling, preserving and generally making herself anything
which would cost even a halfpenny less than the shop version,

she contrived to give us a standard of living which put to shame many of our better-paid but careless neighbours. At one stage she even set her mind on piano lessons for me, although any capable music teacher could have told her I was virtually tone-deaf, and I joined the comparatively select ranks of local children who had music lessons. What this cost her in house-keeping ingenuity I shall never know.

My father never found it easy after the War to make friends, and doubtless any kind of entertaining or social life would have been economically difficult for him. To go into a public house for an evening's drinking was unthinkable for him, and I believe it would have destroyed his self-respect entirely to have gone into the Working Men's Club which was immediately opposite our house, and from which nightly came the noisy joviality of many of the families in our street. Only a very limited number of our neighbours could expect to be greeted by him, and for the most part he lived in a withdrawn world which scarcely touched the world of our street. He rarely, if ever, talked about his work, and until I was twelve or thirteen I had singularly little idea of what he did or how low was his status.

Above all, perhaps, my childish belief that we were superior to our neighbours was fostered by an awareness of my own precociousness. I knew perfectly clearly that in the Infants' and the Junior Schools I attended I was easily the best in the class. I was the one who went out in front of the class to tell them stories. I was the one the teachers liked. I have no idea how obnoxious this may have made me, but in fact I was only once bullied, when I was about nine, and although at the time the campaign of persecution seemed to go on for ever, it must have been quite short-lived, and came from one individual boy. Generally the rest of the class accepted me as a tolerable eccentric who occasionally paid worthwhile dividends in the shape of stories instead of sums. Once I moved into the 'Scholarship Class' at the age of ten I was one of the pampered and protected élite.

Each year about a dozen started the course. About seven or eight were finally entered for the examination, and usually two or three at most passed. Tommy Whitehouse, the Headmaster, was a man of the old school. He had been jumping children through this hoop for many years, and he knew his stuff. He taught us everything himself, and he drove us hard. He very rarely used his cane on the scholarship class, but he stood over six feet and had a powerful voice: his very presence and the righteousness of his anger at any backsliding made a cane superfluous. Beneath his authority he was a kindly man. He escorted us personally to the examination centre, and he kept our spirits up all the way, and comforted us for every recollected slip on the way back. But I think he regarded rote learning as the highest form of human activity, and we went from him, whether failures or successes, very little more educated than when we first arrived. For me passing the scholarship was another precocious trick which I found pleasantly easy, on a par with my stock turn at family parties of reading at sight any part of a newspaper put into my hand.

Culturally, up to the time I passed the scholarship at eleven, I was in another no man's land, but again with nebulous pretensions to something better. To the best of my knowledge my mother never read a book, and she looked at the very occasional woman's magazine which found its way into the house only for the practical purpose of finding a knitting pattern. Even the Bible was something for her to listen to in Chapel rather than to read at home. She took no interest in local or national affairs. Her whole life was bound up in her home, her family and the Chapel. She had four sisters and two brothers, all married and with families, and all living within a radius of a mile or so. Almost every day, one or other would 'pop in' to our house, and every Sunday evening there was an unvarying reunion. Those who went to Chapel would do so, and then 'pop in' on the others in turn, collecting a sizeable covey of relations, Pied Piper fashion, who would go for a short walk and then gather at the eldest sister's house for gossip and sometimes home-brewed stout. At Christmas these reunions spread to include relatives from several miles away, and the Christmas and Boxing-Day parties were red-letter affairs for us children. My mother was strongly determined to do all she could for me, but she saw her contributions essentially as domestic and practical, making it poossible, by shrewd budgeting, for me to have whatever I needed. She was the mainspring of our household.

My father was the passive partner, falling in with her suggestions and backing her, but rarely if ever originating a plan. Yet quite unintentionally he gave me something she could never have given, a love of reading. His sole enthusiasm was football and in particular Wolverhampton Wanderers. His weekly visit to the Molineux ground was an immutable ritual. My mother and I would meet him after the match, combining the visit to Wolverhampton with shopping, and we would return home to a special Saturday high tea—kippers were a favourite item. Then we spent the evening round the fire with Saturday Night Music Hall on the wireless as the highspot. During the evening my father would re-live the afternoon's match, or get his vicarious thrills if it had been an away game, in the pages of the 'Pink 'un', the local Saturday evening sporting paper. Although I never remotely equalled his interest in football, I also read the 'Pink 'un', cover to cover, from a surprisingly tender age.

Every evening my father steadily read his way through the Wolverhampton *Express and Star,* and every Sunday the *Sunday Dispatch.* In addition he usually read two novels a week, either Westerns or detective stories. For the most part I think his reading was purely escapist, filling sizable gaps in his remarkably empty life. He never seemed to vary the diet, he never discussed either the books he read or newspaper items, and he never urged me to read for myself. Often my mother would accuse him of being 'dead to the world with your nose stuck in a book', yet behind her chiding lay a note of admiration for an achievement which for her was incomprehensible. I rapidly assumed that reading was manly, cheerfully risked the same forgiving rebuke, and was soon reading everything he read. By the age of eleven or twelve I must have read a couple of hundred of his novels, and although it was hardly ideal literary fare, it provided me with a reading fluency and a vocabulary which gave me a flying start in the Grammar-School. In those days, too, before children's comics became predominantly picture strips, there was plenty of solid reading matter to be found in the *Wizard, Hotspur, Skipper, Rover* and *Adventure.*

Oddly enough, considering the other things they let me read, my parents regarded these as 'trash' and never allowed me to buy them. Even more oddly, once I smuggled them into the house after swapping marbles or conkers for them, I was allowed to read them if I kept them decently out of sight. In this surreptitious manner I read my way through vast quantities of them.

Obviously nobody moulded my reading habits. I never had stories read to me at bedtime, and the children's classics remained for me to discover when my own children came along. In one unplanned leap I plunged into reading and found myself simultaneously reading voraciously on several widely differing levels. Mixed in with the staple diet of newspapers and my father's novels there were the childish Richmal Crompton 'William' books and fully adult travel books. Tibet, I remember, was one passionate preoccupation. From a session with semi-illicit *Wizards* I would turn to *The Illustrated News History of the 1914-18 War*, twenty-two impressively bound volumes which filled up the only bookcase we had in the house. Undeterred by the fact that I had neither the space nor the money to embark on even the most modest layout, I consumed book after book on the building of model railways. Gradually, as I found out how to use the School Library and the Public Library, some degree of selection took place, but as nobody at school before the Sixth Form advised me what to read the selection remained distinctly erratic. I remained ignorant of whole areas of likely books, and I constantly read books far ahead of my understanding. At about fourteen, for example, I read every word of T. E. Lawrence's *Seven Pillars of Wisdom*, although I had only the faintest glimmering of its real significance.

Nevertheless that book was a turning point, for it led to my first speaking engagement. The Chapel ran a weekly evening in the winter months when visiting speakers or leading members of the group delivered papers, and with the brash confidence of my Grammar-School status I offered to do one on Lawrence. I can still remember the polite disapproval of the elderly Secretary who proposed the vote of thanks, for in my youthful audacity I started the talk like a sensational newspaper with the moment of Lawrence's dramatic death on the speeding motor-cycle. I think this was my own idea, not one borrowed from any book I had read, and it threw me back twenty-five years with a jolt when I found a recent film version employing the same device.

My mother died suddenly at the early age of thirty-nine of a cerebral haemorrhage, and for a time the firm domestic background which had sheltered me disintegrated completely. Deprived of the driving force which had kept him going ever since his war wounds broke him physically and psychologically, my father shut himself off from life entirely, except for the absolute essentials of going to work and eating meals. His whole being froze into helplessness, like a man who had suffered a crippling stroke, but he retained enough of his faculties to realize fully his impotence. In a different class situation he would have retired to a nursing-home with a nervous breakdown, and a housekeeper would have been imported into the home. But the one did not come within our scheme of thinking, and the other was economically extremely difficult. For a time the strain on me was intense, coinciding as it did with beginning Sixth Form work, but after a few months I coaxed back enough initiative for him to accept a radical solution. Instead of getting in a housekeeper we went to live in the house of a widow with three children, who could look after us. This both removed the purely practical problems, and gave him a chance to recover psychologically away from a house and district where memories constantly rubbed him raw. He subsequently married the widow and she lavished love and later nursing attention on him. Despite increasing chest trouble, which seems to have followed from war-time gassing, his last years were remarkably peaceful and happy.

From the time of my mother's death I was very conscious of going it alone. My mother's affection for me had been strong, but the Puritan in her disapproved of outward shows of affection. Emotionally and intellectually I was already moving away from her before her death prematurely broke the link. By the time my father was re-settled the Second World War was upon us, and three years in the Army followed by four years at University made my visits home infrequent, and further thinned the tenuous bonds between us. Even before my mother's death the dominant factor in my life had become school, and from the moment I brought home the Greek alphabet to learn as homework the gulf between me and my parents had steadily widened.

It was a good school. It not only had a history going back to 1515, but its sense of tradition and purpose was alive. Some of this impressed me unduly, perhaps, because it was my first conscious encounter with living history, but to my youthful imagination Stephen Jenys, the local lad who had made his fortune as a Merchant Taylor and become Lord Mayor of London, still seemed very much in evidence on Founder's Day, keeping a firm and approving eye on his 'fre Grammer Scole'. The sheer size of the place, especially Big School where we had Morning Assembly, greatly impressed me after the cramped and dingy 1870 Board School I had attended. I was blissfully unaware that this Hall was mock-mediaeval dating from exactly the same period as the Board School, and regarded it as the pinnacle of architectural achievement.

Initially the strange new subjects, Latin, French and especially Algebra, and the unaccustomed challenge from twenty-nine other bright scholarship boys in my form, reduced me to nightly tears and desperate prayers. Fortunately there was a system of Monthly Orders, and after four weeks I was reassured by coming first in most subjects, and all my worries disappeared. For the rest of my time I felt that door after door was being opened for me leading to hitherto unsuspected treasure rooms. Somewhere about the Fourth Form I realized there could be a grand climax for me, summed up in the magic word 'University'. At that stage this Eldorado had no precise meaning for me. Each year a certain number of the god-like Sixth disappeared towards it, and we all clapped heartily when their awards were announced. But except for the staff who taught me, I knew nobody who had been to a University, and I had only the haziest of notions as to what went on there. Generally I took it to be a straight extension of school life, and for me that was incentive enough.

Some of this idyll was real. Warren Derry was a fine Headmaster and in his prime when I passed through the school. In my experience he is unique amongst Headmasters for I have never once heard anything but praise for him from his staff. Indeed, several who went on to headships themselves paid him the great compliment of borrowing his ideas and even his details of organization. He attracted a first-class staff, and the Classics side especially was very strong. Looking back I recognize that while the school was very good of its kind, the kind was conventional in many respects. As in many similar Grammar-Schools, craft subjects, Art, and Music had almost token existences, and even Geography rapidly disappeared from the timetables of academically able boys. At Sixth Form level Maths was respectable, but Science was very modestly provided for, and English, History and Modern Languages were heavily overshadowed by Classics.

I now realize, too, that probably a good deal of Common Room discussion lay behind my progress up the school (I learned later, as a temporary member of staff during a University vacation, that detailed personal dossiers were kept for the pupils), but at the time everything seemed to happen automatically and with the minimum of consultation. When the first major decision came at the beginning of the second year I simply found myself specializing in Classics. At the other end of my course the choice of Oxford was just as automatic: I was simply told I was being entered. In this respect my school life was less an academic breakthrough than a comfortable ride on a smooth-running escalator.

Adding colour, stimulus and excitement to this well-ordered journey were any number of staff who sparked off latent enthusiasms or created new ones. There was Charles Race, who treated his second-year Form as though they were already undergraduates. He could communicate enthusiasm to that age-group about the layout of a mediaeval monastery (the only teacher who ever explained the lavatory arrangements!) as well as when he made dry-as-dust Antiquities periods come alive for the Sixth. Somehow—illictly, I suspect from a timetable point of view—he introduced us to Psychology and a whole range of other topics. Sometimes the duller patches of Higher Certificate set books would be enlivened by J. D. Eastwood's accounts of his University escapades, which gave us something of the flavour, if not always the sober facts of University life. Above all for me there was R. L. Chambers, who set his mark more firmly than anyone else on my personality and intellectual interests. Not even he could make me a first-rate classicist, although it was not for want of trying on his part, but he taught me more than any other teacher about how to think and how to express myself.

Not all the impact of these men came within the classroom by any means. Often it was in School Societies and in odd informal gatherings at their homes that the lasting influences worked. Typical of this was a passion for acting which I caught from W. H. Bailey, a teacher of French who was later killed in action in the Mediterranean. He brought bounding energy to anything he tackled, and not least his play productions. He was friendly with professional actors at the local Rep., and some of them joined us boys from time to time for play-readings at his house. Doubtless every repertory actor cherishes the belief he is another Olivier, and doing Shakespeare, even with a bunch of schoolboys, must have been a relief after twice-nightly West End farces. These readings immediately acquired a new dimension from the professional seriousness and expertise they supplied, and although I have seen many versions since, my definitive Hamlet is still the one done at this time by an actor already too old for the part, whose name never reached the West End. For me, striving consciously to create a personality out of a mess of very raw material, acting offered a wonderful opportunity for experiment. For the space of the rehearsals I could try on and discard personalities as I wished, yet the text and the producer kept any one version comfortingly coherent.

Oxford was a great disappointment. In fairness I must say it was post-war, austerity Oxford. A wave of students released from the Forces in August and September 1945 broke upon the Colleges well ahead of the younger returning dons who were still serving or working in Government Departments. Elderly dons brought back from retirement stemmed the flood at many points, and their Edwardian attitudes consorted ill with the Brave New World I was looking for. One particular antediluvian tutor wasted an appreciable part of every meeting I had with him bemoaning the iniquity of allowing women

35

into the University. Everywhere accommodation was very short: sets of rooms became bed-sitters, and the queue for meals in Hall was often so great that it was preferable to go out to a war-time British Restaurant. Undergraduate society was a strange mixture of ex-Wing Commanders with wife and three children in a hell of a hurry to get a qualification and a job, and medically unfit boys fresh up from school.

In any case I was expecting too much of Oxford, and expecting the wrong things. My schoolboy hopes had been inflated enough, and the long boredom of unexciting Army service had inflated them still further. During long night-shifts doing Intelligence office work I had built a personal heaven among the dreaming spires. Nobody had told me that the Oxford principle was, and still largely is, to give its students unlimited freedom, including, if they wish, the freedom to make a complete mess of things. Significantly Oxford dons still talk of 'men' going up, regardless of the fact that only a few short weeks before they are boys at school. Although the Army had done much to mature me in some ways, I was still very much a schoolboy in my attitude to studying and organizing my own time. After the spoon-feeding of school and the regimentation of the Army I was totally unprepared for the casual, gentlemanly, dilettante attitude epitomized in the postcard I received only a few days before going up. It emanated from the Dean and asked: 'By the way, what do you propose to read?'

It took me some time to realize that I was off the school's escalator and very much on my own. Probably this difficulty faces all students going up to University, today as then, and irrespective of class background. However, my impression was that Public School boys coped better. Housemasters and other staff seemed to have done more to bridge the considerable gap between Sixth Form and University, and because of this or because going to University was an accepted part of their social milieu, they knew what to expect of Oxford, knew where to look for it, and generally settled much more quickly to getting the most out of the University. I spent too much time groping, failing to realize, for example, that if I wanted to make a mark as a debater I had to join the Union at once and work my way assiduously through the hierarchy of offices. I

DEREK DAVIES

also found it hard to deal with College servants, and remained apologetic and deferential to the end. Otherwise my background made no difference. Some working-class students paraded their origins aggressively and developed an inverted snobbery. Most fitted unobtrusively into Oxford life, and established Oxford institutions accepted them unquestionably. The dons readily took up anybody with brains and an interest in their field, and undergraduate societies—with the exception of anachronistic select Dining Clubs—accepted talent irrespective of background. In this very significent way Oxford's offer of freedom was thoroughly genuine. Other aspects of Oxford I found very much less genuine. I kept an occasional book of quotations at this time and looking through it again I am surprised how often I noted a quotation to pin down some feeling of mine against Oxford. For instance, to Oxford's penchant for wit rather than worth in its flood of talk, I see I have applied, with several triumphant exclamation marks to point the aptness, a remark at Gladstone's dinner table: 'Hunting for epigrammatic ways of saying what you don't think'. Again, my reaction at that time to Oxford dons and their vaunted scholarship was summed up in a quotation from a Professorial Inaugural Lecture:

I feel, and I feel it happily and proudly, that we are all in the game together. But what are we in it for? Is it, after all, just an enormous academic diversion?[2]

I found nothing in the rest of the lecture to alter my youthful opinion that it *was* all an enormous game, played by overgrown children, and added my private comment at the side: 'The awful possibility! All honour to him for voicing it!'

Obviously I sampled only a limited range of Oxford dons, but one encountered honourable exceptions. A tutorial with A. J. P. Taylor was always immensely stimulating, and his lectures, which attracted maximum audiences at very unpopular hours on Saturday mornings, still seem to me to be models, learned yet lively, wide-ranging yet strictly disciplined, and

[2] Christopher F. C. Hawkes. Inaugural Lecture on his installation as Professor of the new Chair of European Archaeology, November 1947, Oxford University Press.

always provoking the student's own thought. Similarly I often cut my History commitments to listen to C. S. Lewis lecture on English topics, and I admired the scholarship and the humanity which took him in his writings from literary criticism to science-fiction novels, and from theology to children's stories. But for the most part the dons struck me as a poor lot. Their lectures were often dull and badly presented; their teaching was confined to recommending a list of books to read; their preoccupation with research smacked of esoteric hobbies and, judging by the amount some published, downright laziness; and their academic feuds seemed to be petty in the extreme.

Perhaps for my personal emancipation there was little left for Oxford to do. I had already seen my vision when I first began to be invited to the homes of the school staff. There I found, often without being able to analyse consciously the components, a style of living which rapidly became my ideal. There was talk and argument, and books and music, and pictures on the walls that clearly did something more than merely fill up a space. Their rooms seemed twice as large because nobody had crammed in masses of useless furniture. The wives seemed to be equals with the husbands, and both treated their children as rational and responsible creatures. I had no doubt that this was what I wanted.

Equally I had no doubt that education was the career for me. My motives were mixed and by no means all fully worked out when I first voiced the decision. The main influence was obviously the staff I so admired. Their lives and their jobs seemed to be closely bound up together, and I could not see myself having the life without the job. At the same time I was influenced by the working-class assumption, still remarkably common today, that teaching was not only the best opening for a bright lad but the easiest, offering clean hands, short hours and long holidays. Without for a moment having religious or political convictions I also felt increasingly that what education was doing for me it could do for anybody else. It simply seemed self-evident to me that precious few of the children from The Black Piles got this chance, and anything that could be done to increase their chances had to be done.

And so, when I was asked in the Fifth Form what I wanted to do, I went the whole hog and replied with radical enthusiasm: 'Take the educational system of a town and reform it.' Even after experience taught me that it is governments and administrators rather than individual teachers who change systems, it has remained a remarkably sustaining aim.

III

G. HENTON DAVIES

Principal, Regent's Park College, Oxford

Twelve miles north of the beautiful city of Cardiff lies Ponty-
pridd where the main Rhondda valley and the Merthyr valleys
meet. Three miles further north in the Merthyr valley is Aber-
cynon where the Cynon valley joins the Merthyr valley. Eight
miles north of this the narrow valley suddenly swells into a
large basin, and in this basin lies the town of Aberdare, locally
styled 'The Queen of the Valleys'. Here in 1906, I was born.

Early in the nineteenth century my father's family had moved
into Aberdare from the Vale of Glamorgan for the opening
of the collieries and the various 'works', the iron and tin
foundries. My father's father died of consumption in his forties
and left grandma to rear a family of two sons and several
daughters. My father's family did not play a very great part
in my life, although I am still in touch with some first cousins
on that side. My mother's family of rural tailors likewise came
with the 'coal rush' from the Crescelly and Llandissilio districts
of Pembrokeshire. One of my mother's ancestors was Mayor of
Pembroke during the Civil War. Still earlier two young male
Hentons were conscripted from the parish of Carew to serve in
one of the Crusades.

The main influences in my early life are through my mother's
side. Her father, Benjamin Henton, also died of consumption
in his early forties, but he had managed to make his mark.
He was a traveller for a brewery firm, although himself a
staunch teetotaller. He was the secretary of the Central Welsh
Baptist Church in Aberdare. He was also one of a small group

of men who set up in business as the 'Aberdare Co-operative Society', to fight the exploitation of the miners in the public houses and company shops of the time. He also paid a visit to America, perhaps to visit a group of Hentons who had settled in Kansas, whose members bore the same christian names as did the Pembroke-Aberdare group.

His untimely death left my 'gran' destitute and with four small children. Gwilym, Edith (my mother), Edward and a baby, Arthur. She began to let rooms to lodgers and to take in washing, and presently married again, this time to one of the lodgers. He eventually became Grandfather to my brother and me. Through this marriage 'gran' was enabled to raise her family, and give her children a start in life. Gwilym went into the bank and leaving home used to send his mother a few shillings a week until he married. He retired as a Bank Manager having amassed nearly £40,000 during his lifetime. My mother learnt dress-making but lived quietly at home with her mother until her marriage to my father. Edward, the most remarkable of all, was apprenticed to an architect, and eventually became an architect himself, remaining a bachelor all his life. Arthur became a solicitor in Bridgend and built up a good practice, enjoying a wonderfully happy married life. Unfortunately, unwise speculation in a derelict brickworks brought him eventually, during the South Wales depression of the 1920s, to bankruptcy and suicide. He died childless.

My father's elder brother died in his youth and so father became his mother's sole support. His mother's dependence upon him meant that he had to postpone his marriage. It happened that he was gifted with what became a most remarkable tenor voice, of exceptional tone and quality. He once sang as a youth in the Market Hall, Aberdare, before 8,000 people, with his back to that great audience! The next day plans were initiated in the town to raise a public fund to send this boy away to the Royal College of Music, but he declined, not being prepared to leave his mother. His singing is still remembered in Bethany Methodist Chapel in Aberdare, where he could lead and outsoar the entire congregation. I often heard him say 'My Hymn Book is my Bible'. Certainly it was the only book he had ever really mastered. There were few books in our home, although my father was very proud of a set called *The Horse*. He showed these to callers, but I do not think he had ever read them through. My mother also read very little, but they knew Handel's Messiah, Judas Maccabaeus, Mendelssohns' Elijah and other oratories off by heart. The constant struggle against poverty, and the goal of a week's holiday by the sea every year, precluded the purchase of books.

My father started work in a local foundry at twelve, but soon transferred to a colliery five miles from Aberdare, as a measurer underground. He remained with this firm through many vicissitudes for the next fifty-nine years. Through all these years he caught a train at 7.45 a.m., and then later at 8.15 a.m. When he was at last promoted to cashier, he travelled first class, but by car on Fridays, taking the 'pay money' for the colliers from the Midland Bank in Aberdare to the pit, safeguarded by a policeman wearing a revolver which was not loaded.

My parents, before they were married, used to live in adjacent streets, and they frequently saw each other, although he was a Welsh Methodist and she a Baptist. Mother used to say she disliked father for a long time. However, the young people from the chapels were wont to holiday in New Quay, Cardiganshire, and during one of these holidays my parents really got to know each other and later married in 1904, when he was thirty-five years of age, and she thirty, after a fairly long courtship. My mother several times testified to my father's pure approach to her during their courtship.

When I was born, father was still a clerk at twenty-five shillings a week, living as he did always in rented property. At my birth, for most of the time of her pains, my mother was alone in the house, help only arriving just before I was born. Five years later my brother was born, but miscarriages prevented further additions to our family.

In 1913 when I was seven, a large house in the locality— Craig House—became vacant, and because times were hard it could neither be sold nor rented. As a favour to a firm of solicitors who were trustees to the estate, my parents went as caretaker tenants for a few weeks for a few shillings a week. Yet there they died, mother nearly thirty years later in 1942, and father six years afterwards in 1948. For all these years the rent was never raised but father maintained the property and the extensive gardens, paddocks and field of four acres. Mother's step-father and other workmen had free allotments and in turn tended the gardens and supplied us with vegetables. The house was never modernized and the kitchen flagstones had to be sanded and the kitchen grate blackleaded every week. The running of that house meant drudgery and a slavery from which only death relieved my mother. The memory of this house remains one of the abiding influences of my life. It was a large house by valley standards with four living-rooms, five bedrooms and with very long passages up and down. We had not had a bathroom and indoor toilet before. For many years we lived in the back rooms and the two front rooms commanding extensive views were set apart as the best rooms. Gradually they were furnished, but they were not used. Then one day Mother explained to us that we were moving into the smaller of the front two rooms for a few months, while the back living-rooms were redecorated. This move also meant that we would 'dirty' the wall paper in the front room preparatory to its re-decoration. In fact the few months did not come to an end, and we continued to live in the front. The rambling spaciousness of the house in which my brother and I had separate bedrooms was a pleasant background to youth. The house was very hard on my mother. In virtue of his job my father had free coal and this ruled out the use of gas or electricity except for lighting. Each morning my mother rose, cleaned out the kitchen grate, lit the fire, cooked the breakfast and got my father off to work before 7.30. Once a week that terrible grate was blackleaded. Twice a week the stone floors were scrubbed and sanded. Every Thursday mother made the bread for a week. Hers was a life of unending toil, yet in the evenings she gave herself to embroidery, and I still possess some of her embroidered panels, cushions, curtains, pictures and the like. My father was 'out' nearly every night of the week. At first he was concerned in the activity of the Liberal Party. Later he became a member of the Committee and then Chairman of the Aberdare Co-operative Society. At first he had been against the 'Co-op', but my mother persuaded him to take an interest. In turn it meant many lonely evenings added to the days, for my father worked six miles away from home.

Our house was perched on the south side of the valley and commanded extensive views to the north and north-west. Just over the Merthyr mountain on the opposite side of the valley could be seen the two peaks—the chair—of the Brecon Beacons. I must have seen these nearly every day of my life and they glistened white in the winter snows. When we used the garden lavatory we could see through the cracks in the door the Black Mountains in Brecon and Carmarthenshire twenty to thirty miles away.

I went to the Council School, and won a scholarship to the Aberdare Grammar-School. When I told mother the result she was so pleased, she would not believe me. Memories of these school years are not very numerous, but inevitably some are dominant.

My particular friend was Albion Treadgold, but in spite of his striking name, I lost touch with him after leaving the primary school. We used to pick football teams from each class on Mondays, and the particular game would last through all the playtimes until Friday. You may imagine the pandemonium of perhaps three prolonged football matches all going on to-gether in the irregular school yard with a bottle neck in the middle, amidst scores of other boys and girls at play with other games. No wonder there were accidents, quarrels and often fights. In our classes too, boys used to group in pairs, the brainier member of the pair to help with homework and sums, the more brawny to undertake the frequent fights for both partners. My 'protector' was Tom Lidiard, a loyal friend and a most doughty fighter.

After school hours we used to play and race on the steep mountain slopes of the 'Craig', behind our house. We would divide into teams, one occupying and defending 'the flat', a small space the size of a tennis court, where we often also played football. The other team would attack from below and eventually from above. We used to gather piles of small stones for attack and defence. We became wonderfully good in aim, but even more quick-sighted and agile to avoid the falling rain of stones.

I used to walk for hours on and all over this mountain until I knew, and still know, every inch of it. I can remember too the exuberance of running and leaping for sheer joy of living along the rocky paths. How sure-footed we became because of these fast runs and long and high jumps along the lovely mountain side.

I remember too playing as left back for my school in the primary schools' 'soccer' competition, held in the public park before a sizeable crowd of miners. I believed that as left back I was only permitted to kick with my left foot. I got so tired that I decided to have 'a go' with my right foot, and hoped the referee wouldn't notice.

Our form-master in the primary school was a man called Richards, and to him I owe one enormous debt. He gave me a love of reading and of wide reading too. He, himself, was a superb reader, and our all too frequent request was 'Sir, please read to us'. I can still remember him, reading to us as a class, in the winter afternoons, sometimes as long as half an hour after normal school hours. We hung on his reading and on his interesting summaries of the dull bits in between. We were regaled with *The White Company* and the like, various poets, Norse Mythology, Dickens, Henty. That teacher in the Council school in Foundry Town had a great influence upon me. In later years no matter how specialized my reading had to become, I have clung to my conviction that I should always read as widely as possible. Thus I have always tried to parallel my Old Testament study with comparable reading in classical studies, and my debt to Bowra, Kitto, Nilsson and others is very great. Similarly, too, I find constant refreshment in Jane Austen and Anthony Trollope, having read and now possessing more than forty of the latter's novels.

One school memory is outstanding. We boys were sometimes guilty of hanging round the school toilets and returning to class late. One morning a group of us returned late, and teacher Richards admonished us and then caned us in front of the class. As the last boy was being caned, the Headmaster, W. Notton, walked in and enquired the reason for the punishment. Richards explained. Notton then applauded Richards, and turning angrily on us, said that such conduct must stop, and began to administer a second round of caning. I immediately blurted out, 'It's not fair, we've been punished once.' Richards bade me be quiet, but when my turn came I refused to give my hands to the Head. He began to hit me with the cane over my head, shoulders and body, but I refused to give my hands. He hit all the more and I received a terrific thrashing before a spellbound class. I was then put back in my seat, but a few moments later, when the coast was clear, I ran out, and after dinner hid in a hay loft until afternoon school was over. When I got home at tea time my parents knew all about it. Next morning my uncle Edward, the architect, took me back to school, and we went into the Headmaster's room. 'Well Notton', said my uncle, 'what's all this trouble about?' I still remember the shock of realizing that anybody could talk to a Headmaster like that. Thereafter I lost all respect for Notton, and despised his bullying.

Out of school I was also involved in a rumpus in a hayfield. My father's first cousin, Willie, had a large family and worked as a collier at night, and a small farmer by day. He was an honest, very hard-working man, but he expected everybody else to work with equal vigour, whatever their strength. He was particularly hard on the horses drawing the mowers, rakes and haywains, and used to beat them hard with whips, sticks, pike handles, anything to hand. One day I was goaded into remonstration. He laughed at me, and beat the horses again. So ten years old sailed into thirty years old. I was picked up and handed to my mother. In a few moments I stole Willie's whip and ran off with it. I destroyed it, and returned to the hayfield. I admitted that I had removed the whip, and refused to say anything about it. All the workers were with me, but they feared Willie too much to say anything. I do not know whether Willie was kinder to the horses thereafter, for I was not allowed to go to the hayfield again that summer.

Years later Willie and his sons were at work underground. A stone fell and killed his son, Glyn, at work by his side. The stretcher and the ambulance were so slow in coming, and Willie was a strong and impatient man. He picked up his boy's dead body, slung him over his shoulder, carried him out of the coal 'level', and in the middle of night he carried his son home several miles. Arriving at the farm he called out to his wife, 'Maggie, O, Maggie. Come down at once; Glyn has had an awful 'urt.'

There was another event. My step-grandfather developed a cyst on his back, and entered hospital. He was the last, or almost the last, to be operated upon that day. The local hospital was small and the women patients were complaining of the smell of gas. This news came to the men's ward and my grand-father heard it. When his turn came he refused the gas anaesthetic. He lay down on the table, and for an hour endured in silence without so much as a sigh or a sob, whilst the surgeon removed the cyst. He simply said he didn't want the women to have any more of 'that gas'.

These heroic chapel men, for whom the chapel was their sole solace, often went down the pit before dawn, and came up from the pit after dark, their women in dread all the day long. Some owners had their 100 per cent profits from this sweated labour. Like other children I used to visit the sweet-shops to find out from which shop, and what kind of sweet I could get most for a halfpenny per week pocket money. I had to wear boots till long after they were too small for me, and my toes are still bent as a consequence. A favourite phrase of my mother's was 'pinch and scrape'.

We had a very happy and delightful life at the Central Baptist Chapel. The regular worship, the Sunday School classes, many of them with their grammar-school boys and girls, the religious and social life, the discussions on religion, politics and almost everything except sex. Our teacher, Jean Owen, was a very progressive and modern Sunday-School teacher, and she opened our eyes to the Bible, to ethics and plain, honest, good and beautiful things. In the Sunday-School we reached a depth and a variety in discussion which was never approached by anything in the Grammar-School. There was also great preaching, and the visits of great preachers twice a year. The Ministers who served the Churches in the valleys were almost all of them College trained and many of them were learned in Hebrew and in Greek. Several of them were graduates and double graduates of the University of Wales, and there was also a sprinkling of men who had been trained, not only in Wales, but also in Oxford and Cambridge. One of these men taught me the elements of Hebrew and another helped me to begin the study of Greek. This was the quality of ministry which we enjoyed in those days in the Valleys. The Church was peaceful too, ruled by James Griffiths, our pastor for forty-two years.

Only one man gave some anxiety. He was David Richards, a man of great natural eloquence, but who tended sometimes to sulk. In spite of that we were all fond of him and were proud of his oratorical gifts. Like so many others too, he was gifted in prayer. These colliers taught me the reality of prayer.

Our chapel was the Welsh Baptist Church and 'mother' of some twenty causes in the valley. From our chapel came too the English chapel, Carmel. This church was not so peaceful, and during the First World War, a group of the members 'withdrew' on the 'pacifist' question, and founded a new English cause, 'Christ Church' a mile or so away. Among that group were numbered my own English-speaking step-grandfather, the hero of the hospital story above.

It follows that Sunday was the happiest day of the week, so full of activity with the young people in church that there was no time to want to do any of the forbidden things. Not to be allowed to bathe in the sea on Sundays on holidays seemed to us to be the only grievous limitation. Although the chapel was really a strict Baptist Church and only those baptized by immersion were allowed to partake of communion, the deacons and the elders were broad-minded in other ways. For example the Chapel owned a recreation ground furnished with a brick pavilion, two 'En Tout Cas' tennis courts, a grass lawn meant to be a bowling-green and a children's playground. The young people did not gain this without a struggle, for some of the older members thought it was wrong for the Church to provide facilities for recreation and sport. The majority of the Church members were for the young people and eventually gave or raised the money to buy and furnish the ground. The Chapel's recreation ground on week days was a centre for tennis and friendship and marriages! Unlike H. A. L. Rowse who testifies to his unhappy Cornish childhood, my chapel-centred boyhood was a creative, joyous and disciplinary experience for which

I am profoundly grateful, as I am proud of those who brought me up.

One evening at the recreation ground when I was about twelve years of age, I had a remarkable experience. One of the tennis players, Eddie Jones the Chapel organist, asked me to take care of his spare pair of spectacles while he played a few sets. After a few moments I chanced to put the glasses on, and suddenly saw a new world. I had been short-sighted all my life without realizing it. I suddenly saw the mountain with new clarity. I rushed round looking at the distant vistas with astonishment and rapture. I was really seeing distances for the first time, and my life was altered. Soon I had my own spectacles and have been careful ever since to have my eyes tested at regular intervals. Parents, teachers and friends had completely missed this important weakness in my physical abilities.

Apart from my parents, the chief influence in my early life was my uncle, Edward George Henton, architect, artist, Sunday-School teacher and philosopher. He was an extraordinary man, and in fact may rightly be called a genius. He owned one of the first motor-cars in Aberdare—a Hermes-Mathies, I think it was called. He took it down and re-assembled it. He decorated the ceiling of the chapel with many colours. He gave talks on, and made models of, molecular structures. He was learned in Greek philosophy and English literature, especially Shakespeare. He was the friend, companion and tutor of a select number of grammar-school boys and girls. He and I went for long walks and I heard long monologues concerning the stars, astrology, literature, and philosophy. His erudition was enormous and his interest unfailing. When I announced my intention to enter the ministry, he developed an interest in the Bible and theology. This eventually became his sole and abiding interest. He had read through Hastings' *Encyclopaedia of Religion and Ethics* and most of the *Britannica* as well. My debt to him in knowledge, discussion and perspective cannot be calculated. His library I still enjoy.

After gaining the scholarship I went for four years to the County School in Aberdare. On the whole my teachers were competent and adequate but not one of them ever really captured my interest and imagination. I got by in English, History and French, became interested in Latin but did not care for the sciences or mathematics. No doubt during these years text books were my principal concern. Nevertheless my memory is a complete blank as far as the reading of books is concerned. I cannot recall any recommendation of books, and I cannot recall reading any book of any kind that enthralled me. Whereas previously in the primary school the teacher had fired our imagination with his reading, and whereas during the two years in school in Cambridge that followed my four years in the local Grammar-School, I was fired by the works of Warde, Fowler, Lowes Dickinson and Livingstone and others, these four years are a barren period as far as books were concerned. Similarly in my first year at the University J. R. Seeley and other writers maintained the fire, and ever since then the worlds of literature have slowly yielded their treasures.

I qualified at sixteen years of age for matriculation, narrowly missing a distinction in Latin. The night before the Latin examination I read through almost in one sitting the first four hundred and eighty-six lines of Book Two of Virgil's *Aeneid*. In the next twelve months I was to read all twelve books and begin Greek. But Greek never appealed to me as Latin did. My mark in Physics was only eleven per cent. The chemistry master, 'Doddie' Elliot, a completely disorganized teacher, divided his class into 'non-donkeys and donkeys'. The former would pass and the latter fail the matriculation examination. Several of the 'non-donkeys' actually did fail, but I remember that I was the only 'donkey' to pass.

Two years still separated me from University entrance. My parents discussed at length with my uncle what I should do. Fortunately, although it was unbearable at the time, they decided to try to send me away to a Public School for a couple of pre-University years. Because of their tenancy of the house at a peppercorn rent, because of the frugal habits of my parents, and because of my mother's tremendous capacity to save and, above all, because of a deep conviction about education and the necessity of educating their children at all costs, they had begun to accumulate a little money to pay for the education of my brother and me. After several unsuccessful applications, they eventually found a place for me under Dr. W. H. D.

Rouse in his classical sixth at Perse School, Cambridge, where the direct method was practised. I began the study of Greek, gained several prizes for Latin orations in Virgil's *Aeneid*, but after five terms, began, to Dr. Rouse's great disappointment, to prefer Hebrew to both Latin and Greek. On the whole these two years at Perse School, Cambridge were probably a mistake. They launched me into a classical sixth, and a famous one at that, but without the school experience necessary for it. Besides I was in the midst of a pilgrimage which was taking me through French and Latin to the Biblical languages. Perhaps the emotional upsets due to leaving home, which did not last long, helped to shape my thinking in the following months. Certainly my horizons were broadened, and I was soon to discover my life's work, but my two years at Perse were not particularly happy. I was dubbed 'Taffy' and teased because of my Welsh background. I joined the O.T.C. but as soon as they began to teach me to shoot I went on strike on religious grounds and joined the 'non combatant' weaklings and nitwits. The teachers were naturally much more exciting and I remember particularly Appleton, de Glehn and F. C. Happold. But even they were all overshadowed by the dominating figure of W. H. D. Rouse of whom I was very fond and for whom I always had great respect.

My father's minister, the Rev. R. Richards, initiated me into Hebrew. In the winter of 1923/4 two events took place which altered the course of my life. The first event was a discovery. One day I caught myself discovering a sentence in my head: 'You are going to be a minister'. I was completely astonished and my parents even more so. My father wished me to be a doctor and a surgeon, a desire brought about no doubt by the many deaths among the menfolk of his family; my mother hoped I would become a solicitor and enter her childless brother's practice. But it was not to be. The sentence just quoted has dominated my entire life, and from time to time in moments of personal crisis and decision has served as the final guidance.

As a first step I applied for baptism and at seventeen years of age I was baptized by the rite of believers' baptism. This prescribes that those who request baptism, as Jesus Christ himself did, and make this request upon confession of their Christian faith, are totally immersed in water. Those baptized are laid down in a pool of water as a symbol of their death to the former life, and then lifted up as a sign of their rising to a new life. Once on their feet they are turned round and walk out of the Baptistry at the exit as opposed to the entry.

Having been baptized, I refused at first to join the Church. My reason for this was I felt that the Church like all the other local Baptist Churches was wrong in closing its communion table to all Christians unless they had been baptised by immersion. In other words Christians of other communions who had only been christened as babes, and not immersed at their own request as adult believers, were not allowed to come to communion. I argued at that time that however logical and correct the doctrine was, such practice was really the failure of Christian fellowship. I registered my protest by refusing to seek admission to the Church membership roll. I persisted for nearly one whole year, and only gave way when I discovered that my plan to train for the ministry could not begin until I had joined the Church. Mine, even if one of the first, was but one of many protests, and rigid rules have largely broken down today.

In all this my parents took the part of observers. They counselled me and tried to understand me; on the whole they were patient and extraordinarily tolerant. The toleration, common sense and good humour of my father were beyond praise. My mother, more intense and anxious, scolded and yet supported me. Always they stood by me even when they were convinced I was wrong, and in fact was wrong. Out of the mists of those years have come again in recent years, re-emerged in the memory, three texts of which my mother was very fond and to which she was herself personally committed. When I left home in my late teens she quoted to me:

'My Son, if sinners entice thee, consent thou not'. (Proverbs 1: 10). Nearly twenty years later I chanced at a provincial University Senior Refectory Table to sit next to a man who was a very eminent figure in the world of science. He was a professor and I an assistant lecturer. He was kind to me and questioned me as to my name and subject. When he discovered that I taught Hebrew and Old Testament he told me that he had a son in Australia, and that that very morning he had written to him suggesting he should read Proverbs 1: 11 and other passages from chapters two and five and seven. To the learned professor's astonishment I immediately quoted Proverb 1: 11 to him and went on to identify the 'harlot' passages from the other chapters to show that I had understood the drift of his advice to his son. So the science professor in the great University and my humble mother in the Welsh valleys had the same advice to proffer.

A second text was in Psalm 37 which opens with some verses of exceptional power and some verbs of great tranquillity 'Fret not', 'Trust', 'Delight thyself', 'Commit thy way', 'Rest', 'Wait patiently'. My mother was especially devoted to verse five of this Psalm:

> Commit thy way unto the LORD;
> trust also in him
> and he shall bring it to pass.

and she commended it to me. Presumably my mother found it fulfilled in her experience; certainly, hitherto, it has been fulfilled in mine.

The third text, also from the Old Testament, was from the prophecies of Hosea:

'Break up your fallow ground', part of verse twelve in chapter 10. The prophet's words in my mother's voice had remained an abiding challenge. These verses serve as an illustration of the legacy of my home, a parental deposit in my spiritual bank account.

An event of importance to me was my father's loss of all his money because he had gone guarantor for my mother's luckless solicitor brother, who became bankrupt and then committed suicide. I had to cancel my place at Queen's College, Cambridge and entered University College, Cardiff in 1924 to read Philosophy. My mother paid both my fees and my digs out of her housekeeping and savings. I began about this time to take *The Times* which I have read ever since. In 1925 I was admitted to the South Wales Baptist College, Cardiff to begin training for the Baptist Ministry, and changed also from the Honours course in Philosophy to the Honours course in Hebrew. The lecturer in Hebrew was Theodore H. Robinson, shortly to become one of the most famous teachers and students in the field of Old Testament study. In 1923, however, his students were so few that the University authorities had to warn him that his department might have to be closed. In 1924 Aubrey R. Johnson, eventually to be Theodore H. Robinson's successor in the chair of Hebrew created later, and about another dozen of us, were admitted as students. The department never looked back. In 1927 came the first 'first', J. C. Jones, later Bishop of Bangor. In the session 1927 and 1928 the number of students had so greatly increased that Johnson and I were both teaching second-year students and sitting the final Honours examination. Johnson and I both took 'firsts', and he switched to classics and later to research at Oxford and in Germany. I did the Master's degree with distinction in Old Testament theology in 1928/9, and in 1928 H. H. Rowley was appointed a lecturer in the Department.

T. H. Robinson took me aside to tell me that H. H. Rowley had been appointed, because I had been on the short list, and then he said to me 'But remember, there's always Bristol'. He was referring to a Tutorship in Old Testament Studies at Bristol Baptist College. Eight years later when that tutorship became vacant because of the resignation of F. E. Robinson, a saintly man, I was appointed to the vacancy. So my official teaching career began. After thirteen happy years I was appointed First Professor of Old Testament Studies in the University of Durham.

The years between 1929 and 1935 included two years' research at St. Catherine's College, Oxford for the B.Litt. on the 'Idea of Covenant in the Old Testament'. Dr. G. H. Cook and Mr. Stenning of Wadham were my examiners. During the 'viva' the former remarked that he thought I was not very clear about the chronological order of Ezra and Nehemiah. I took the cue and meekly submitted my ignorance, whereupon to the visible disapproval of Stenning he spent almost all the rest of the viva putting me right.

After the completion of my Oxford B.Litt. I went to Marburg/Lahn in Germany to read Rabbinics under the Jewish teacher, Dr. Bialblocki. When I arrived there I learnt that the

Nazis had just removed him from his post, and so I continued
with more conventional Biblical studies. It was my good fortune to hear Karl Budde's very last course of lectures. These
lectures were on the text of the Minor prophets. I also heard
Bella's lectures, but he was a stupid Nazi who abused
his students with his insolence. Rudolph Otto came into
the lecture theatre fifteen or twenty minutes late, spoke
for about fifteen to twenty minutes, and then left. His
class might just not have been there. He appeared to have
lost interest in teaching and in students. By contrast the lectures
and personal interest of Heiler and Bultmann were highlights
of my stay in Marburg. Von Soden and Frick were also interesting. Bultmann of course was the chief centre of interest; he
taught one the strength and the weakness of Form criticism,
but I was really too early for his de-mythologizing aberations.

My sojourn for two semesters in Marburg gave me great
insight into the differences between German and British
scholarship in the field of Old Testament studies. The Germans
led the field in original insight, innovations in methods of study
and in the presentation of new theories. Their suggestions were
often ingenious, captivating but almost invariably exaggerated
because of Teutonic thoroughness. 'I have proved', says the
German Professor to you. The result is, of course, that professors of theology, especially if they are young and inexperienced,
as they quite often are in the Seminaries in the U.S.A., I
afterwards discovered, fall victims to the latest German
hypothesis. To British scholarship must be accredited the distinction of being not so easily carried away, of assaying and
discovering the excesses of German theory, and of recovering a
saner, if duller, outlook.

These years of study in Oxford and Germany were con-
ducted on a shoe-string. Before the end of my second semester
I had to tell Professor Bultman that I had no more money and
had to leave two weeks before the end. I had my ticket home,
and arrived in Cologne with one mark only in my pocket. I
spent nine-tenths of it on a pork chop, and left the one tenth
as a tip. I journeyed from Cologne to Cardiff on the strength
of that pork chop. I carried a suitcase and walked from
Victoria to Paddington. I literally did not have a penny left

in the world. My fiancée lent me my bus-fare to Pontypool the following Sunday. There at Trosnant Baptist Chapel I received twenty-five shillings for the day's preaching, and I was quite rich again.

Altogether I was a student for eleven years, and for most of that time my parents were down on their heels. From 1924 onwards after entering Cardiff Baptist College, I received free University tuition and maintenance grants. A University studentship saw me through 1928-9 and to my M.A. A Dr. Williams' Divinity Scholarship saw me through Oxford and Germany, helped by a scholarship given to me by the Baptist Union, after I had failed their examination twice. I refused to sit a third time, and presented the files and notes which I had prepared for the examination. When the Baptist Union officials saw the work I had done, they gave me the scholarship without more ado. Sometimes examiners not only in denominational circles, but in University examinations as well, simply do not understand what is required in setting an examination paper.

During my two years at Oxford, 1931-3, at St. Catherine's, I was also a member of Regent's Park College where Dr. H. Wheeler Robinson was Principal. This College gave me small terminal grants of money to supplement my divinity scholarships. Altogether my eleven student years cost about £1,800, financed mainly from my mother's gifts in the first year, free living at home during the vacations, scholarships and awards and preaching fees from the Baptist Chapels in South Wales, to which I have always owed so much.

Saintly parents, who endowed me with a reasonably healthy body, an eccentric but learned uncle who vastly enlarged my horizons, a primary-school teacher who gave me a love of books, a chapel and a denomination which in spite of all their faults and failings and their low rating in social status have largely satisfied me, membership in four universities, and teaching experience in two others as well as Oxford, all these together with a happy married life, have given me a wonderful breakthrough into a full life, which I hope has been of some use to all the generations of students to whom almost my entire life has been given.

IV

SHEILA FELL

Artist and Lecturer, Chelsea College of Art

Cumberland is a county of sloping hillsides, mines and farm-steads, with the wind blowing in great gusts across the miles of bare earth. The village of Aspatria, surrounded by fields of barley and potatoes, lies in a hollow within five miles of the sea, the mountains nearby. Fences, back-to-back houses, strips of land divided into allotments and a long tape of a road leading from the woods on the outskirts up past the gas-works to the cemetery and the market square or Beacon Hill as it is known locally. In this village I was born. . . .

When I was a child, the industrial collieries around Aspatria, with their chimneys, winding houses and slag-heaps all huddled together, were still functioning. The inhabitants of the little rows of dwellings worked either in the mines or on the land. The life of the village was punctuated, day after day, by the ritual going to or coming from work. I can remember watching the miners strung out along the road or crouching on Walter Wilson's corner with bait boxes, shivering against the morning cold. Farm carts, ricketing past the house, full of hay or turnips, and cows threading their way from milking sheds to grazing fields; and then in the soft black evenings, when one by one the lights would glow from the windows of the houses, the next lot of men would turn out for the night-shift, everything silent except perhaps for the moaning of the wind blowing from the sea across to the mountains and the stirring of cattle in the barns. The trees near our house would sough all night and often I would hear the warning cry of a bird. I used to lie in

57

bed, feeling tremendously secure, thinking that I wasn't that poor night-bird being chased by its terrifying enemy.

There was an old man who coughed very loudly, and in the darkness, running with my mother's shopping I often nearly jumped out of my skin if that loud, sharp bark of a cough sounded through the blackness. It was always a glorious thing to come into the warmth of the kitchen, safely back in the light and the smell of food: my mother moving briskly from room to room—all the lozenge shapes, dots and daisy patterns of her aprons glowing in the light of the fire.

At this time we had gas-light in the cottage but when I was put to bed at nights, I had an oil-lamp placed on the floor in the corner. It shone on the red eiderdown of my bed and made it seem to come alive and move: the room would be brim-full of shadows and I'd just be able to recognize, lying back on the goose-feather mattress, the shapes of the trinkets on the dressing-table: small white pots laced with patterns of violets and a huge jug and bowl with kingfishers painted on them. We had a glass case filled with artificial flowers and fruit. I loved the cornflowers and cherries best. Lying underneath the foliage in the glass case was a small white, naked baby made of, I'm not sure what, wax or pottery. I was never allowed to remove the glass to touch it and find out in case I broke it. I slept in the back bedroom where the Family Bible was kept, full of pressed wild-flowers, and my father's black box of ebony hair-brushes.

The front bedroom was my parents' room and above these two rooms ran the attic, long and low with a skylight and pale-washed walls. In the evenings, it would be full of sunlight and the smell of fruit, as it was here my mother kept Christmas apples laid out on long sheets of paper and the yearly hoard of pickles, chutney and jam. There was some of my Grand-mother's furniture up there too. Dark brown glossy chests-of-drawers with wooden handles and a huge bed with a wrought-iron headpiece decorated by round brass knobs, in which I sometimes slept if we had guests. My great grandmother had made the feather mattress and she had left her bodkin inside it. On the ground floor was the kitchen where we lived and ate, it's window overlooking a little yard with whitewashed walls.

Here, we had a huge Victorian open fireplace and chunky black oven. On the days my mother made bread and teacakes, the oven would roar while the white dough in it's stone pot stood in the hearth growing bigger. On one side of the kitchen was the scullery containing a vast iron set-pot and stone sink; on the other, the front room with it's big cosy armchairs, rugs and the organ rising against the wall, tall and sombre with black and white knobs, yellow teeth and red-carpeted pedals. My mother had bought it before she married and was able to play it quite well.

At Christmas time, she would always be totally preoccupied with the making of plum puddings, mince pies and spiced meats. I loved it then. We would feed the wild birds before dark, throwing crumbs on to the roof of the woodshed and I would sit in front of the kitchen fire on a brown leather fender-stool and watch them through the windows swooping down out of the cold sky. Sometimes, my mother would feed them on her own and I'd watch the reflection of the light shining in the dark glass of the window and onto her face, frowning slightly, her arm making a black bar, rising and falling into and away from the round, bright, reflected light sprinkling crumbs to the fluttering half-forms scanning the top of the woodshed.

Down the hill between Millers Farm and the Primitive Methodist chapel is a row of cottages and I was born in the front bedroom of the second one, just at the time when my father was out on strike. He was working at No. 5 pit one of the Brayton Domain Collieries owned by a Mr. Joseph Harris of Carlthwaite Hall and situated about a mile and a half outside Aspatria along the Cockermouth Road. No. 5, the youngest of the pits was sunk in 1910. The workings were in the Yard Bank seam but in this pit the coal was much deeper and the seam only thirty inches thick. From 1932 onwards men were paid off in small batches and in 1936 my father along with the rest was out of work. The Union money was no comfort; it was so little. The vast unemployment and poverty of the twenties with endless strikes for better conditions in the mines had depleted the funds; they were worn out. After a time he managed to find work again at 'Slowly On', a drift pit a few miles outside Aspatria. He needed to buy a bicycle in order to get to work and managed to obtain a second-hand one for twenty-seven shillings, paying it off at a shilling a week. By the time he had finished paying for it, the drift pit had closed upon being declared unsafe and once again he was out of work.

I would be about five years old by this time and although I was never conscious of it, the five years must have been difficult ones for my mother and father. My mother had made a lot of my early clothes from decorated petticoats and nightdresses which had been part of her trousseau and as she had learned tailoring as a profession before she married, she was was able to make some extra money by taking in sewing. I was an only child and spent most of my time with my mother, as my father always seemed to be at the pit or in bed sleeping between shifts. I have recollections of the deep cupboard by the kitchen fire, where amongst other extraordinarily exciting things such as tins of polish with twiggy metal openers on the side, was my father's flannel pit shirt and shorts rolled up and huddled into the fire wall.

At the age of six I contracted diphtheria. My mother refused to put me in hospital as she'd always had a deep distrust of them so I was confined to this room for seven weeks. She collected rolled-up leaves from the blackberry bushes in our garden and inside each one would be a tiny patterned spider. She used to bring them into the bedroom heaped in her apron and throw them onto the bed for me to open. The variety of these spiders' colours was a constant source of anticipation with the unrolling of each leaf. Hard blue ovals, delicate green, pink or lemon smudges scrawled with thin lines, luminous and strange they ran over the coverlet of my bed. A quite different experience about this time, which awakened my imagination was the opening up of a Norse tomb, in which a seven-foot long skeleton was found.

My mother had a treadle sewing-machine and apart from the whirring noise it made day in and day out, the atmosphere of the house was peaceful. Nearly all my time was spent with my mother and as she spent most of her days at the machine, it played a large part in my life. It was very ornate, and reared up like a little black horse with a tight garland of frosty green and gold flowers printed on it's side and a silver hand-wheel, the whole, standing on a mahogany cupboard affair with long narrow drawers full of bobbins, silks, elastics, and all such bright and wonderful things. Supporting this cupboard was the underbody, weaving itself like dark glossy liquorice into elaborate legs, large wheel and treadle. While my mother was hand-stitching or cutting, I was allowed to sit on the treadle with the mahogany roof overhead and make the wheel go round which moved me and the treadle to and fro. I don't know which I found more exciting, these rides or the beaded silks-basket. The silks-basket was circular and ancient with tiny beads running around it, the red ones shining like berries on a Christmas hedge, the more acidly yellow and green ones glittering secretly against dark static blues.

Then there was the button-bag with a drawstring top, made out of butcher's apron material and faded underneath the navy-and-white folds into a gentle mauve. This was bulging with buttons of every shape, size and colour and kept me busy on many a long winter's afternoon. We used to empty it out into a noisy clattering heap on the kitchen floor: big brown dignified lozenge-shaped buttons, tiny white baby ones with delicate daisy faces printed onto them, buttons like foxes' heads and glinting metal suns, little twinkling diamantés and sober fawn overcoat buttons trimmed with pale lilac heather. There were recognizable red Scotch terrier shapes, just off a summer dress know as 'the doggie dress'. The fascination of these buttons lasted long after I started school and my mother used to tell me the history of each of them as we sorted through the pile. The stories were always exciting and funny and I believe she enjoyed telling them as much as I enjoyed listening. I was allowed occasionally to accompany my father when he went to his pigeon loft which was in Holliday's field, opposite the house but I was usually taken very quickly back to my mother in disgrace for being a nuisance and disturbing the birds. He has always been very proud of his pigeons. Most of the miners in the village either grew flowers, as did my grandfather, who had a genuine love of his garden; kept greyhounds or flew racing pigeons and cared for these things in an instinctive and intuitive way.

The pigeon loft has been there all through my life, white-washed and clean with its small square nesting boxes mathematical and precise as a Mondrian painting, except for the bright eyes staring from each cube and the light grey or chocolate forms with awkward scuttling feet and beautiful strong wings. I used to watch the shaggy babies perplexedly learning to bath or take corn, but I wasn't allowed to move for fear of frightening them. The whole mystique of the pigeon clocks in their square yellow boxes, the little silver numbered rings circling the pigeon's legs, brass thimbles and packets of faint fine paper dials scored with pink lines, sheets of pedigree in my father's sloping copperplate handwriting and his regular disappearance to a place called the pigeon club fascinated me and I determined to find out what it was all about. I followed him one night when my mother's back was turned, up the village street, past Miller's farm and the school into the courtyard of the Brandraw Hotel where he disappeared up some old stone steps and through a battered door. I did the same and found myself in a large dismal-looking room with hundreds of strange masculine faces all turned in my direction. I wished I'd never left my mother and especially when I saw my father advancing towards me. The punishment was to return home alone without his comforting figure walking ahead.

At the age of five, I began to attend the village school. My mother took me down the garden path and told me to go with the other children who were passing our house; I ended up in a pleasant room with a rocking horse, sandpit and coloured rush mats on which we all slept in the middle of the morning. My school life was uneventful and what I can remember most vividly from this period were the mornings in winter when I was awoken. There was always the feeling of earlier activity about the house: my mother would often be up at four to light the boiler or see my father off to work. We'd have breakfast in the kitchen, the chimney yawning like a black cavern at the back of the unlit fireplace but the bright, fragile gas-mantle would send a cosy glow trembling across the tablecloth and plates. My mother with a long plait, which she'd not had time to pin up, made treacle animals and birds on my slices of bread. She'd dip the spoon into the dark treacle and twirl it around, then we'd wait as it came down with a quick plop onto the bread magically forming itself into a bird, a pig or a rabbit. It wasn't hunger that made me eat three or four slices: it was that I couldn't bear not to see another shiny creature appear on yet another piece of bread.

Then with Spring everything opened up. The mystery and terror, sudden warmth and snugness of dark nights, would vanish and the hedges around the village be laden with blossom. Spiky crocuses shone through dark tufts of grass like neon lights and the last of the single pale wintry flowers gave way to huddles of sulphur coloured primroses, dog-violets and tiny cold faces of blue speedwell growing secretly in woods. I went to school in the mornings between the cool patches of sunlight feeling glad and excited: determined to give my mother no rest from the long nagging till I could wear a cotton dress. As summer grew, there were the lanes to explore, no longer muddy and bleak, but dusty and warm, heavy with the smell of meadow-sweet and blackberries. After school, we'd search for fat blue bilberries, staining our mouths and fingers or sneak through the corn and wheat fields, hoping the farmers would not catch us, leaving long snaky paths of lopsided grain in our wake and filling our pockets with hard little kernels picked out from the husk to sustain us till supper-time. We'd spread out over grass fields, looking for mushrooms and I can vividly remember the excitement at seeing a round glossy white back embedded nearby. As a last resort, there were always the shiny sour dock leaves to eat in great jaw-locking mouthfuls. But the evenings were just not long nor light enough and we would arrive home full of a sense of guilt, due to our dirty state, and despondency, because the day was over.

Just after starting school, I began to have music lessons at one-and-threepence a time and went once a week to the little back room of a sweet shop nearby where I began to learn to play the piano. The smell of sweets, dolly-mixtures and caramels, wafted through tantalizingly while I practised the scales. There was also a Wednesday dancing class which cost one shilling. My mother's sewing paid for these and sometimes I'd hear the machine going in what seemed to be the middle of the night.

When the 'Slowly On' pit closed down, my father was again
on the dole and, unable to find work near home, he was forced
to take a job in Whitehaven, a town on the coast roughly thirty-
five miles west of Aspatria. He had to move away from us
and go into lodgings in Parton, an old colliery village close to
Whitehaven. Parton consisted of rows of old-style miner's
cottages built on a hill right against the sea; tunnels had been
cut into the hillside, under the streets of grim little houses and
these tunnels led onto the bleakest shingle beach I have ever
seen. One could stand on the shore and watch the cold Solway
lapping against the desert of rocks and coal-coloured sand with
a view of tall chimneys further around the coast. My uncle
Joe, my mother's brother, once took me down when the fishing
boats were coming in and I was given a herring by one of the
fishermen. There was something extraordinarily poetic about
the existence of Parton: a pit village closed in on itself, it's
inhabitants and looking out to sea. It has all been pulled down
now but I always approach the place with feelings amounting
to awe.

My father lived in Parton for two years, only coming home
at weekends, accompanied by my mother's brother, a sort of
free-lance pitman with a team of men who travelled around
contracting to different mines in Cumberland. They had the
repuation of being very strong and quick workers. He and my
father would bring with them crabs, shrimps and mussels, as
my uncle was friendly with the local fishermen, sometimes
rabbits or hares and coloured rings for me. Friday nights
sharply contrasted with the sort of peaceful closeness which
had existed between my mother and myself during the week.
They were gay and bustling, full of adult conversation and the
preparation of food. Then one day the pit caught fire, at least
the face they were working on did, and there was a terrible
scramble to get out for fear of explosion; the coal-face was
sealed, the men paid off and the trek for work began again.
The years at Whitehaven had been headache years for my
father who not only had to send money home for us, but also
had to pay his lodging there, so things had been very short.
My mother, during what must have been rather lonely week-
days, sometimes had a friend to stay, a terrifying old lady whose

visits I simply dreaded: she didn't like me much either and told me one day when my mother was out and I'd been misbehaving that when I died I would go to Hell, ending her proclamation with a description of how it would be. This made a tremendously fearful impression on me, nor could I ask my mother when she returned as she'd then know of my misdeeds while her back was turned. I remember feeling completely isolated and aghast for hours afterwards, walking around the garden being depressed by the wet blades of grass and no-one to turn to. But when my father arrived home at the weekend, he said nonsense to it all and my world readjusted itself.

Especially while he was living away and right through my childhood, my mother and myself would visit Broughton Moor, where she had been born and where most of her relatives still lived. This was a windswept village with huddles of low straight cottages lining the long sloping road and the thin old church standing at the crossroads, reaching up to the light, the whole, surrounded by lonely stretches of heath scrub dotted with wild gorse and one or two overgrown mine shafts. Often, just after I was born, she would take me wrapped in a shawl across three miles of moorland and fieldpaths, after the bus set her down at Maryport, to stay for a few days with her mother. The life of Broughton Moor was far more closely knit and rural than that of Aspatria. Children were an integral part of it, much as they are in Latin countries; there was no keeping them out of anything, for they sat at every hearth joining in every activity and conversation. Families were interwoven and the whole community lived in close contact with each other and to the chapel or church. The dialect was broader, and 'thee' or 'thou' was used more liberally.

As I grew older I enjoyed and looked forward to these visits. We would call on different friends and members of the family, go up steps, along passageways and through gates until it seemed my mother must know every single person behind every single door.

In the top part of the village lived a very close friend. Her daughter and myself would play in their huge garden called 'The Planting' which was full of clucking hens and sweet peas: at one end was a sun house crouched into shadows thrown by tall trees, at the other, a small clay pit. Using an accumulation of flat stones and pieces of wood, we would make scores of minute clay cakes or buns and decorate them with flower heads. The sight of those grey cakes moulded and finger-printed into sturdy squares and rounds, with their great variety of patterns and decorations gave me the most enormous satis-faction. By the wall which ran around The Planting, climbed a red briar rose which my maternal grandmother had planted as a seed just before she died when I was two years old. She had been buried in Aspatria and once a week my mother and myself would take the shears by their yellow wooden handles, a large bunch of flowers, and walk up past the cypresses and elms to the back of the church.

I liked the cemetery, it had a rolling hillock at one end dipping into a hollow where there was a well embedded like a green toad, magical and old. My job was to go to this well for water, while my mother trimmed the flowers. All the dead blossoms from the graves was strewn into the hollow, its banks seemed to be lit up with yards of narcissus, hyacinth, iris and white, startled heads of lilies carefully bound by fragile wires into springy moss, forming circle or cross shapes. Sometimes there were little sympathy cards, gently attached, their ink already smudged by the rain and wet grass. Searching up and down the slopes, I'd be aware of two things—the presence of the vicar looming blackly in his vestry who might come and interfere at any moment, and the fact that my mother would be growing increasingly impatient wondering where I had got to with the water. Near to where she was always occupied stood a young stone angel rising from the green ground, whose aloneness and perfection caught my imagination. Some old bricks set into the encircling cemetery wall were decorated with serpents, birds and odd twisted emblems. Underneath the wall lay stone coffins overgrown by lichen. This strange world fascinated me and I anticipated our visits with pleasure.

My father, after Whitehaven, found work again at Siddick, a small town some ten miles from Aspatria: he stayed there for two years, during which time he had both legs crushed by a roof fall due to rotting props and was rushed to the hospital in Carlisle. After some weeks he returned home moving around rather painfully on crutches. There was an atmosphere of anxiety in the house and frequent visitors. Eventually he was well enough to go back to the pit but after a year decided to give it up altogether.

From the fourteenth century onwards most of my father's ancestors had been farmers around the Solway coast but for one reason or another, the farmsteads had gradually deteriorated until my grandfather at the age of forty was forced to seek employment in the mines. With a family of ten children to support, he was obliged to take an auxiliary job as a gardener when his shift was done at the pit, but he had tremendous vitality and was still recklessly bicycling in the face of all traffic when he was eighty, convinced that the white line in the middle of the road was his prerogative. As pillion-passenger on the back of my father's motor-bike he sat with watch in hand, determined they would make good speed.

My paternal grandmother had died before I was born but I remember my grandfather; he would nurse me in front of the fire whenever I visited him. My father was the fourth child and began in the mines at the age of fourteen with a wage of six shillings a week, threepence kept off for the union and threepence for the doctor; he worked on the top amongst the tubs for six months then went down. The First World War began and when he was twenty, he went to France with the Border Regiment, first to Mons then Vimy, St. Omer and eventually Ypres, where they helped to dig the first line of trenches around the town. In 1916, wounded by shrapnel and with one of his lungs badly burned by chlorine gas he was invalided out, sent back to England and hospitalized for seven months after which time he was recalled. Not being fit to go back to France he returned, after nearly a year in a wheel-chair, to the Cumberland collieries. The decision to look for an above-ground job had been made because, to further complicate the damage of the chlorine gas, my father had developed silicosis, through continuing in the mines. His first employment was in a flour-mill but later he found work as a police-man at Silloth, a town which, at the outbreak of the Second

World War, had become very active as an air-base and port.

At this time, my grandfather died, having reached the age of ninety-five, and I sat for a scholarship and failed to pass. My mother's brother suggested, that as he was single with no family to support, he would help my father and herself should they wish to send me as a paying pupil to the grammar-school at Wigton, seven miles away. It was decided I should have this chance. The entrance examination successfully passed, all was arranged for me to begin in the September. My mother took a job at the same time, I suppose to offset the difficulties which were to come. Every evening after school I'd alight from the bus at the top of station brow, near the tailor's shop where she worked seated at a long bench surrounded by heavy flat-irons, waxen threads and heaps of corduroy. The room was warm with a coal stove at one end and an odd glimmering light which seemed to focus itself on baleful shapes of dark cloth hanging bat-like around the walls. Tea was brought in for us and there were always delicious little cakes. At six o'clock we'd make for home to prepare food and light the fire before my father returned. This new pattern, although lacking the previous close warmth, was varied and exciting. I became an avid reader and searched around not only in the school library where the choice was wide, yet invariably I seemed to come away with adventure stories, bright and new, aggressive print jumping off every page. Amongst the shelves at home the scope was very narrow but I obliged myself to read more seriously: the books with their old Victorian covers and faded sepia inscriptions carefully bound, much used and familiar seemed to have a sense of history and reality about them which those at school did not. My parents had collected Burns, Gray and Oliver Goldsmith and also there was a big tome on the social revolution in Russia with lots of fiery illustrations. What interested me most were the small silken-coloured flags and emblems attached inside it. A large green book contained an extraordinarily grave and beautiful story 'The Foundling of the Fens' which I read over and over again. There was in addition the family Bible. A religious sect called the Plymouth Brethren were in the habit of calling around the village to hand out leaflets about resurrection, heaven and hell. These leaflets were decorated with the most devastating pictures and I'd sit by the fire, adrenalin racing, absorbing them with a sort of fascinated horror.

Through the school, there came the chance to go to Holland for two weeks on a children's tour. I had never been away from Cumberland in my life and it wasn't Holland that impressed me, but the journey home when our train arrived in Westmorland. The mountains, after the flatness of Gelderland seemed to force themselves, black and hostile almost through the window of the carriage. Slab over slab they rose up and enveloped us like a gigantic frightening wall nearly touching the glass and shutting out the sky. They hung over the train like great forlorn prehistoric animals and although I'd lived among them for years, it was the first time I ever saw them.

Eventually I took the school certificate and passed, then stayed on and on in the sixth form not quite knowing what to do next. The art teacher, whose enthusiasm and interest had influenced me a lot during my years there, wanted me to go to the art school in Carlisle. The headmistress felt I'd do equally well at languages and also be more secure. My parents didn't know what to do for the best (I didn't) and said they felt unable to interfere. I had to make the decision. At the end of a worrying six months, I travelled the twenty miles to Carlisle, holding a large portfolio. I was interviewed and shortly afterwards, almost before realizing what had happened, had begun to embark on the course which was later to lead to London.

My first day at art school was spent in a cold depressing room, surrounded by stuffed birds in glass cases and black printing-presses, copying a basic design carefully from a book. The other students seemed so sophisticated and terrifying I didn't dare speak a word to anyone. Full of disappointment and wishing I'd never gone, I travelled the twenty miles home to spend a tearful evening in front of the kitchen fire vowing to my mother that I'd never stand it. Gradually, I became used to the place and continued laboriously working on classical designs of acanthus leaves or Persian birds in thickets. My solace was the library, situated right next door, where I could browse through books throughout the lunch hour and also during the tea-break before evening class began, then return home at night with an armful and settle down after supper to read. Lives of painters, sculptors, poets and books on their work led me, in order to obtain a sense of time or relationship, to-and-fro, through a maze of history, philosophy and geography. These things, in their turn, led to others; avid with curiosity I determined that as soon as the first part of the diploma was completed—if it were possible to obtain a grant—I'd make for London. Over the years, plodding on with my piano lessons, I'd become familiar with the music of Scarlatti, Mozart and Bach and had also had the chance to see the Rambert ballet company at Whitehaven, where I sat breathless, while the glittering bird in *Peter and the Wolf* fluttered its wings out of fear. For a month or so afterwards, the borrowed books were about ballet and the theatre. There was so much more than this, impossible to describe, which caught my imagination and increased the desire to find out further.

During the years at Carlisle, the financial position had been tense. I had been given a grant to cover fees and bus fares but for some reason although the fees were paid, the other was not forthcoming. My parents on top of providing money for materials and luncheons, had ten shillings a week to find for fares which they could ill afford. The years at the grammar-school had used up every penny and my father had been increasingly troubled by a duodenal ulcer which frequently prevented him from working. Finally after making enquiries they discovered there had been an oversight: from then on it was only a question of materials but these could be costly. Anatomy and architecture books I was able to borrow. Trips in a motor-coach around old buildings, such as Lanercost Priory (to aid us with that part of the expected examination dealing with perspective), were out for me and I stayed in the empty school.

At last the Intermediate was taken and passed. With a grant of a hundred pounds a year I set off for London after gaining admittance to St. Martin's School of Art, not encouraged by the staff at Carlisle who thought my talent lay more in the direction of textile design. There was a lot of bustling around at home; books, trinkets and clothes were packed. I had to catch the midnight train and the district nurse was arriving at eleven o'clock to take me to the station by car. We waited, conscious of the large suitcase by the wall, and when she came, the bundles and myself were installed. Then I watched the road become longer as the car slowly moved further away from the dark house with its dim line of cornflowers in the front garden. My parents stood waving until finally I could see only their hands flickering like birds against a night sky and by the time we turned Brewery corner the whole silent village was blurred.

So I settled in London, bitterly homesick for years, dreaming, reading, living on nothing with little food but grandiose ideas, taking various odd jobs, longing for the holidays as all other students have done and will always do. Food parcels arrived regularly from my mother containing meat pasties, gingerbread and hard-boiled eggs. My room cost thirty shillings a week, which only left ten shillings for food, soap, stamps and materials. The teacher at the art school, sick of seeing me wearily drawing, week in week out, borrowed paints and brushes from the other students one day in order to help, which made me feel terribly ashamed and slightly like a charity. Things were difficult at home, I was sent every penny which could be spared but even with this effort it wasn't always possible to keep the wolf at bay. The year I took my diploma at the age of twenty had been a tense one for my parents as my father was taken seriously ill and had been ordered six months complete rest. They didn't let me know about it until much later.

Whereas at the small school in Carlisle there had been a slightly snobbish element, among the students in London I found a creative curiosity and lack of pretentiousness which was positive, alive, and helped to counterbalance the many anxieties. I was granted a post-diploma year but after that, one part-time job followed the other, all unsatisfactory, with never enough time to paint as much as I needed. Released from the Damocles sword of examination I'd worked on some landscapes and slowly, one or two canvases began to mean a little; but it was enough to involve me. An insecure year passed by.

Then Mrs. Lessore of the Beaux Art Gallery saw some of my paintings in a friend's house and arranged to advance money for materials so that I could work for an exhibition.

It all went on from there—looking back it seemed simple even with the complications—I wanted to paint and I did. It was a question of commitment.

V

RONALD GOLDMAN

Principal of Didsbury College of Education, Manchester

Two miles north of Manchester's Victoria Station, and one and a half miles north-east of Strangeway's Gaol lies Lee Road, Harpurhey. It is a row of second-wave Industrial Revolution back-to-back houses, technically a slum, but on the more refined edge of Ancoats, Miles Platting and Colleyhurst. Most of the residents of Lee Road were working-class, but with a fair sprinkling of middle-class aspirants, of whom one was my father.

I was born in the back bedroom of one of these houses in 1922, a second son, my elder brother Sidney being six years old at that time. Upstairs there were two bedrooms and a tiny box-room. Downstairs there was the living-room and kitchen, where we ate, listened to the crystal set and spent most of our time, and the holy place referred to as 'the front room', cold, damp, with a brown substitute leather suite, an aspidistra and an ornate sideboard, a room in which we sat uneasily on Sunday afternoon or on other occasions when we had visitors to tea.

The lavatory, bathroom and a wash-house, where my mother every Monday morning would light a fire to heat the water in the copper boiler, was in the back-yard. Although it was nominally attached to the house, the fact that we had to cross a narrow passage to go to the lavatory inhibited me from a very early age. The house was lit by gas, which did not extend to the outside amenities, and I remember how frightened I was in the dark, having to cross from warmth and light into the unspeakable cold, dark horror. Even with a candle carefully set in a holder on the floor I remember sitting listening to the wind and footsteps up the back passage behind the yard, every sound a menace.

With a shared back-yard, and the front door opening immediately from the front room into the street, I was always conscious of neighbours. Sometimes in the winter, there were unknown visitors who would come down the tunnel, three doors away, and use our lavatory or write rude words on the wash-house wall. This added to my terror, lest I should be in there caught with my trousers down, as it were, when the marauders paid one of their visits. Mercifully, this never happened. In my imagination it happened all too often, as I sat listening for footsteps, as the wind moaned under the door and the candle often flickered out.

The neighbourhood was very close to me as a young child, since Lee Road and the nearby streets were my playground. There was not a square foot of grass within walking distance; everything hard solid brick or cobblestones. My only memories of anything faintly rural were visits by tram-car with my father to the gardens in Piccadilly, Manchester, and to Boggart Hole Clough, the nearest park which marked the northern edge of Harpurhey. I was two years old when we first visited Piccadilly. I recall the tall tulips planted in neat, military rows and the smooth green grass of the lawn laid out with rectangular precision. Boggart Hole Clough was a very different sort of place, with a hill in the centre down which you could roll or run. We visited it only rarely, but it always had a chastening effect upon me because each time I was told 'up the Cluff 'twas where t'boggarts live in an 'ole'. It was explained to me that boggarts were ghosts and were very fond of the trees (the Clough), so I always steered clear of the trees, keeping to the safe, open spaces, except when with my parents or elder brother.

The sounds and smells of Harpurhey and Moston can still be recalled from my first four years of life there. The smell of fish and chips, and beer carried in jugs from the local pub, the hiss of gas-lamps, the quarrels of neighbours or passers-by outside in the street and the distant bell and jangle of tram-cars on the Rochdale Road and Moston Lane. My grandfather was a tram-driver and occasionally gave us free rides right out to the terminus, whenever he was on our route. My memories of these journeys are almost blank, except for grandpa, smart in a dark button-up uniform, flaming red hair, just like my mother's, and nicotine-stained moustache. He was a boisterous Irishman, subdued somewhat in his home, by a slight but prim Scots wife, loving his beer and a good laugh with the boys when he was allowed out on his own. They lived down in Ancoats and I have no recollections of their house. Grandpa was addicted to uniforms, it seems, for his previous job had been fireman at the Queen's Park Hippodrome and he claimed to have been on first name terms with Charlie Chaplin. This was probably part of the Elliot family myth.

There were constant visits by Mother's relatives, especially on a Sunday afternoon. There were two sisters, married respectively to a butcher and grave-digger. The grave-digging uncle was a melancholy type, as befitted his calling, which must have been fairly lucrative, if not thirst inducing, for he was reputed to consume six Guinnesses a day. My mother also had two brothers living, and I remember being told that my middle name, Joseph, was in memory of another brother who had died. One brother was 'in business' and was regarded with a little awe and a great deal of jealousy by the rest of the family. The other brother, tall and slender, like my mother, was always talking about being a prisoner-of-war in Germany. I recall being horrified by the story that their basic diet was potato peelings given them by the German guards. This uncle was a thin, sickly figure, always with a bad cough, selling advertising for local newspapers, doing door-to-door selling or frequently unemployed. He died of tuberculosis and my mother was always frightened that this was a family disease and that she herself would suffer from it.

While on this side of the family there was a great deal of bickering and contention, the situation was no happier with my father's relatives. His parents lived in the most crowded Jewish area of Cheetham Hill, his father a Russian Jew who fled into Poland and married a Polish Jewish girl, whence they fled in the 1880's to England. I have no recollection of my paternal grandfather, who died soon after I was born, but I

75

still recall the slight but bitter voice of my grandmother admonishing my father for having 'left the faith' to marry my mother. We rarely saw her because of this bitterness, for she was an ardent believer. She was a fierce, proud woman who spoke Polish and Yiddish and very little English until her death. The last time I visited her I was a student at Manchester University, thinking of reading theology. Knowing of this she refused to talk to me since this was the greatest betrayal of all, and to my embarrassment addressed all her remarks to me through my elder brother. My father, named Solomon, was indifferent to religion and was not in the least concerned that he had become nominally Church of England, when he married my mother. No one had ever attended Church in our family, except for the normal social and ceremonial events of funerals, weddings and christenings. When my younger brother was born—I was aged nine at the time—my mother felt she had to be 'churched' as a social convention more than a religious act. All three sons were given non-Jewish names, but my father's relatives were populated with names such as Reuben, Rachel, Ruby and Leah.

From my birth certificate I note that my father's occupation was 'designer (hats and caps manufacture)' but this was a little high-flown since he was an ordinary worker in a back street factory in Cheetham Hill at the time, occasionally designing a different kind of hat. He was a restless, ambitious man and I well remember the day he branched out in business, running whist drives in the neighbourhood. It was always an insecure affair, about which mother and father had frequent quarrels. The rows were always loud and long, simply because mother was almost totally deaf, even when very young, and father would shout at the top of his voice to get his points home. Sometimes in bed at night, I would hear them yelling at each other for what seemed like hours, and I would fall asleep with my hands over my ears. Finally, the whist drive business failed, and whether or not official bankruptcy proceedings occurred, I do not know, but we left the district hurriedly to live on the Fylde coast, ostensibly for my mother's health.

During our years in Harpurhey I never recall anyone reading a book, nor there being a book in the house apart from a dusty Bible and a medical dictionary of almost equal ancient vintage. I had cause to remember this book in my early adolescence, when it was handed to me with a marker in the page headed 'Self-abuse'. It solemnly warned me that 'certain habits, if persisted in, invariably lead to loss of physical power and the onset of madness'. So much for my health education.

There was little conversation at home in those early years, except between my brother and myself, partly due to mother's deafness limiting communication and partly due to father's frequent absences from home. There was a radio in the living-room, but it was rarely on because the noise hurt mother's head. Looking back in my early twenties I was puzzled by the fact we never discussed religion in our home, but I later realized it was a taboo subject, and anyway there was very little conversation about any topic, and this was probably couched in 'public language'. Latterly, father became a salesman, as did my elder brother, but father's absences from home grew longer as he began to travel the country on tour with *"Ideal Home Exhibition"* and similar circuses in my late childhood. To my mother's deafness was added my own impediment of vision. My father wore glasses and so did my brother, but no one seemed to spot my difficulty in seeing. Not until I was nine years old did a school medical inspection reveal that I had serious astigmatism. I recall in my early years at school, being quite unable to follow many lessons because I sat at the back of the classroom and simply could not see what was written on the blackboard. I was punished a great deal for simple errors in many subjects and the most frequent phrase used in school reports was 'this child has a lazy mind'. I suppose this was why I both hated and feared school from the very beginning.

Perhaps my poor vision accounted for early perceptual deprivation in some way and the development of an acute sense of smell. Certainly, all my recollections of Moston and Harpurhey were of foggy, indistinct shapes, closed in surroundings and limited horizons. The linguistic deficit also probably had an effect upon my development, and despite my father's middle-class aspirations, the orientation of the home where my mother exerted the most powerful influence, was unmistakably working-class. We were soon to move up the social scale as a family, only to fall back again during the years of the depression. Due either to father's business failure, or to my mother's fear of 'T.B.' and the need to live in an area 'good for the chest', or to both factors, we moved from Manchester to the Fylde coast of Lancashire when I was aged between four and five. We took on middle-class status, renting a semi-detached house, although barely able to furnish it. I remember that almost everything in the house was second-hand, bought at local saleroom auctions, my mother becoming a saleroom addict. While my elder brother was at school I would sit wearily through one auction after another, sometimes sleeping, sometimes watching with detached incuriosity, the long line of wardrobes, china sets, beds, six superb walnut dining chairs, bedpans and every manner of oddment paraded before us. I was mystified by mother's entranced expression, sitting as close as possible to the auctioneer in order to hear correctly what was happening. I think these must have been the happiest afternoons of her life at that time. She was like a person transformed. We would come home carrying the small articles and wait impatiently until early evening when the deliveries of the 'heavy stuff' were made by horse and cart.

My schooldays began miserably, as they were to continue for a long time. We lived opposite the Council School, a 1902 mixed infant and junior structure surrounded by a high brick wall and sturdy iron spikes on top of it, either to keep the sinful world out or the young criminals more effectively inside. I was a shy, retiring boy, too long and too often with my mother to want to leave her. Despite the happy note of optimism sounded by mother about my beginning school I dreaded going behind the high walls and being exposed in the playground to the mass of yelling, running, squealing children. Many afternoons I would creep upstairs to the front bedroom and with my nose flattened against the window I would look down across the street over the wall at the frightening bedlam of playtime. At last the dreaded day came and I sat quaking at my desk, while a fierce, elderly lady with rimless spectacles and a bright blue dress issued us with textbooks,

78

notebooks, pencils, rulers and hundreds of meaningless instructions. Here was no gentle transition or reception class, more like a play-group for a child to enjoy, but full-blooded 'school' where it was obvious from the start that we had to work hard and learn things, although what it was all about completely mystified me.

My sense of timing must have been awry, or my unconscious seized upon a means of escape, for when the bell signalling morning break was rung, and we all poured into the playground, I ran joyously out of the gate and across the road home, convinced that the first day was over. A master, seeing me go, ran after me, seized me in his arms just as I reached the front door, and carried me struggling, screaming and biting back into the playground, carefully locking the gate behind him. This happened again at lunch time and at the afternoon break, ending in the same exhausted, tearful capitulations. But I had one ace card to play. In the final period of the day I defecated into my pants. The smell and the mess was terrible, the gate of the prison house was unlocked and I was led home, at arm's length, by the headmaster. I remember mother dumping me in the bath with all my clothes on, half-angry and half-amused at my predicament.

Unfortunately, the next day was a holiday and the day after that the whole business of settling in had to begin all over again. I am told it took a full week before it was safe to leave the gate unguarded. I gained the reputation with the staff of being 'very difficult and temperamental', a reputation which remained until I left and went to the senior school six years later. Someone may have perceived in those early days how wretchedly unhappy and frightened I was in my first days at school, but I had no tangible evidence of this. My unhappiness and fear turned to hatred and a negative attitude to teachers and to school generally, only tempered by one kind and brilliant teacher in senior school and finally dispersed in university.

Bound up with all this was father's increased length of time spent away from home, louder and longer rows when he returned and with the depression years, a slide from lower-middle-class affluence back into lower-class poverty. Although I was not aware of it at the time this was the beginning of the end

79

of my parents' marriage. By the time I was nine years old my baby brother had been born but my father had disappeared. My mother, frantic and lonely, with very little money, took my elder brother, me and my younger brother, still a babe in arms, on visits to Birmingham, Newcastle, Manchester and London searching the exhibition stands for father. On some occasions she sold the furniture to pay the fares and two weeks later we would return to buy some of it back out of the saleroom. On one visit to London we ran out of money altogether, failed to trace father and ended up in a workhouse. I was probably aged nine at the time and spent two months in a children's home somewhere in South London. Because of age discrepancies the family was broken up, my mother and baby brother going to one institution, and the two boys to another. I still recollect the smell of carbolic soap and stale margarine, the indignity of being searched for fleas and being made to wear dismal grey institution clothing.

Later I was separated from my elder brother, who remained in the men's section. Curiously I had no fears, being taken by a nurse on top of a London bus in the dark for a long journey, until we alighted, walked down streets of decaying houses and we came to the 'home'. I cannot remember its name. It must have been a religious institution of some kind, for my most vivid memory of it was the interminable services we had to attend, two choirboys slowly swinging incense, the first time I had ever seen this, and the sweet smell of it coming from our clothes the rest of the day. This was the first time that I had lived in the South of England, and I often failed to comprehend what was said. During the first medical inspection, for example, I was asked if I had any scars, and I replied saying, Yes, I had a scarf, but I thought I'd lost it on the bus. No doubt I had lessons in this institution but I have no recollection of them. When eventually we were reunited as a family, still minus father, and sent back North by Standerwick bus, it was obvious that my frequent and often long absences from school had left me a long way behind the rest of the class. The class teacher in my old school made no attempt to help me catch up and I remember the total hopelessness of trying to do a long division sum, without the faintest idea how to begin. For this I was clouted over the head, called 'a stupid clot' and made to stay in after school.

From what I have written it might be thought that mine was a totally unhappy boyhood. This was far from true, for I must have had a normal boy's resilience and appetite for enjoying life. Living at the seaside had many compensations and this broad environment, after the restricted brick and mortar of of Manchester, stimulated me in many ways. Almost every day, no matter what the weather was like, I wandered along the beach, sometimes with schoolfriends, sometimes alone, enjoying the pounding of the sea, collecting innumerable objects washed ashore or watching the trawlers steaming past to Fleetwood. I remember happy trips across the Knott End Ferry, and mother, very gay and pretty, buying me my first Peach Melba. There was the annual trip to see 'the illuminations' at Blackpool, the weekly visit to the cinema and the summer pierrot show.

It was at this show I must have overcome my shyness for the first time. They had children's competitions on Friday nights and one epic evening, after biting my nails fearfully outside the tent, I summoned up the courage to sing a song father had taught me years ago. It was a comic song, of slightly dubious morals, sung in lilting comic patter. For some reason it convulsed the audience and I was awarded first prize, a five shilling Marks and Spencer chromium watch. When I arrived home triumphant mother was very worried, convinced that I had stolen it. But taking me back she checked my story and was delighted to know it was true. My repertoire was enlarged, I was coached intensively on Wednesdays and Thursdays, and on Friday nights I stepped on to the platform for my one brief moment of glory, invariably receiving first, second or third prize.

We were so poor at the time it seemed quite natural that the watches should be hocked at the pawnshop or the boxes of chocolates sold to our summer visitors, for at this time our home became a registered boarding-house. I was very content to receive sixpence as my share, knowing the rest went into the family kitty. Total poverty was never far away at that time. I recall coming back once again on Friday with my chromium watch, in a euphoric haze of success, to find my mother weeping on the stairs. 'The bailiffs have been,' she wept, and not knowing what the dreaded word meant I laughed, thinking they were some strange or comic animals. I soon stopped laughing for they had taken every single item of furniture in the house. It was reckoned a generous act to have left us mattresses on the floor and a few blankets.

About the time we came back from London I was presented with a pair of spectacles by the school medical authorities. Immediately, life took on a new and startling clarity. I could actually *see* the blackboard, the pictures on the wall and incredible details never noticed before. It made me more perceptive and my school work began to improve but not fast enough to get me through the 'scholarship' examination for the grammar-school. I well remember the solemn moment of being called into the headmaster's study to be told that my name had been entered for the scholarship. The head, in a burst of candour, assured me I had little chance of getting it, but it would do no harm to try. Not exactly burning with confidence a few weeks later I travelled to Fleetwood, and sat uncomprehendingly looking at the mysterious green scholarship sheets. My memory of the tests themselves is extremely vague but my reactions of confusion I still recall. I had had no practice of speed tests of this kind, no experience of intelligence tests, nor anything remotely resembling them. Not surprisingly, in view of my broken schooling, poor motivation and lack of help I failed to qualify.

So at eleven years of age I proceeded to the local senior boys' school. It was four miles away, and to get me there, my mother bought me a second-hand bicycle. This was a new beginning for me since the bicycle gave me an independence and a freedom I had never known before. The new school, although not madly progressive, had at least two or three inspiring teachers who knew how to get the best out of their boys. It was one of these, a Scotsman, later to move to a teacher training college, who first stimulated in me an interest in books. Until I was taught by this man I had not voluntarily opened a book for enjoyment. In my second year at the school he took us for English, and instead of the dreary analysis of sentences or the equally dreary 'composition' on 'How to mend a bicycle puncture', he actually read stories aloud to us.

Until that moment I had never been read aloud to, not even as a young child, and the pleasure it gave me was tremendous. The first story was George Birmingham's 'Spanish Gold' and we chuckled through the dotty Irish adventures of Thomas O'Flaherty and Thomas O'Flaherty Pat. Then it was John Buchan's 'The Thirty Nine Steps' and we listened intently to the adventures of Richard Hannay. About this time I had attended without a break, a local Methodist Sunday School, for a full year. I was asked to choose a book for an attendance prize and, on the advice of my English teacher, asked for John Buchan's 'Greenmantle'. At nearly thirteen years of age this was the first book I actually owned. I must have read it five or six times. Then with some diffidence, because I had never been in a public library before, I was persuaded to join. I read my way through all the novels of George Birmingham, of John Buchan, of Leslie Charteris (the entire 'Saint' series), and of P. G. Wodehouse. I read, reading for pleasure, thoroughly enjoying the experience, and was soon to learn reading could be used to acquire information, but this was a stage not reached for some time after leaving school.

The remainder of my time at the senior school was very short, since the school-leaving age of fourteen was fast approaching. By this time my parents had decided upon a legal separation, my home circumstances were more settled and predictable, although mother suffered from bouts of restlessness and depression. Since houses for rent at a seaside resort were easy to come by in the early 1930's, this restlessness was expressed in frequent moves to different houses, each one supposed to be an improvement on the last. In four years we moved five times within the same neighbourhood.

At the end of my schooling, barely aged fourteen, I came top boy in all subjects, except Science, in the 'A' class. It is an interesting commentary on the place, an area of seasonal holiday employment, and on the state of vocational guidance at that time, that I was allowed to walk out of the school without a job, and I was thought to be very lucky indeed to have secured, by the next Monday morning, the job of errand boy to a local chemist at a wage of ten shillings a week. Liberated from the classroom, a wage earner in my own right, I turned up on Monday full of expectation. I was speedily disillusioned. Cleaning windows, which mysteriously had more marks on them when I had finished, washing up and sometimes breaking delicate glass beakers or pestles and mortars ('That's one and sixpence off your wages this week, my lad') or pedalling a cycle in all weathers delivering medicines to those too ill to collect them, soon begun to pall.

The one activity which kept me sane during this painful nine months of intense boredom was my elder brother's enthusiasm for rock-climbing. Late on a Saturday night we would cycle north through Lancaster and Carnforth to the English Lake District. There on the crags of Langdale, on Bowfell Buttress, Gimmer Crag and Pavey Ark, in sunshine or pouring rain, I experienced a new freedom. Until I began rock-climbing, sport was one of those wearisome activities imposed by school, yet here was challenge and physical enjoyment of a different kind. After sleeping on bracken in a wayside barn we would arrive home in the small hours of Monday morning, stiff and sore, but ready to start work within a few hours. I dreamt, thought, read and lived for nothing else. I read my way through the local library section on mountains and mountaineering, the Lake District guide books were borrowed continually and almost committed verbatim to memory. This was the beginning of reading for information.

A change of job brought greater boredom but a little more freedom—long weekends to climb the crags—and a doubling of wages. I became a bootboy in one of the houses at Rossall, our local public school. Cleaning shoes all day was somewhat stultifying, especially when one reflected that the boys should have been cleaning their shoes for themselves! But it was my duty as a boiler boy which was my downfall. During my three months at Rossall I don't believe they had hot water for more than a few days. I was shown many times how to remove clinkers from the boiler by a patient housemaster, yet somehow I never seemed to master the technique. It was with something like mutual relief that we parted, I to bottling and delivering milk, the housemaster to a continuous supply of hot water.

After this I spent about three months 'on the dole' in mid-winter when all seasonal jobs petered out. Only a few lucky ones retained regular work. Signing on three times weekly, then lining up for my six shillings allowance was not exactly stimulating, but it gave me leisure to read and I began to work my way along the shelves of biography and autobiography in the public library. This idyllic period closed with my employment by a travel agent, my first white-collar job. At least in this work I did not experience the intense physical fatigue I had encountered in my previous employment. I finished in the early evenings with some energy left for reading and other activities.

About this time, aged almost sixteen, I was taken by a friend to the local Congregational Church. My only experience of religion until this time had been a desultory attendance at Sunday School, and a short but abortive period as a choirboy. I had found the whole experience of institutional religion rather boring and irrelevant, and much to my surprise, I began to attend the Congregational Church with some regularity. The minister was a stimulating speaker with a strong social conscience and his sermons from 1938 to 1939 were topically concerned with war, pacifism, poverty and Socialism. He preached 'book' sermons on *Mein Kampf*, Gunter's *Inside Europe* and other publications.

Connected with the Church was a youth club and I was invited to attend. It was the beginning of a new social life for me, meeting others of my own age, producing, playing table-tennis, dancing. But it was the Sunday night club, meeting after church, which was a turning point and provided the breakthrough I needed. The Sunday evening Youth Fellowships were devoted to discussions and the reading of papers and were mainly attended by fifth and sixth formers at local grammar-schools. For the first time I was encouraged to argue and explore ideas at more than a superficial level, my public language proving so inadequate I had to go to the library and read politics, philosophy and religion in order to be able to express myself. The real challenge came when I was asked to speak the following Sunday, with three other young people, on the theme 'If I were Dictator. . . .' All that week I read and wrote and organized my thoughts and on Saturday I spent the whole day putting it into final form. I still possess this paper, printed in crude block capitals, a full twenty pages of idealism and fervour. Immature it was, but it represented my first attempt to formally present a coherent argument.

This was the time when my education really began, and an acceleration of my thinking was very evident. The club leader and the minister encouraged me to read more by lending me books, stimulating me to attend W.E.A. classes in history and psychology, prompting me to go to evening institute sessions and even to enrol in a correspondence course with the idea of matriculating. Despite further unemployment, and a short time in London on various jobs, I returned to the North at the beginning of the War to start life as a university student, bringing with me the only two serious books I possessed, a Bible and the *Concise Oxford Dictionary*. The War was to intervene and I had a long way to go, but at least I was on my way up the educational ladder.

My entrance qualifications for university were gained with very little insight, and by a maximum of rote learning. I had very little idea what the knowledge I was memorizing was all about, only that it had to be learned. I recall my astonishment when I first began to learn Latin—chosen simply because I could study it by correspondence course and this required no oral skill—that one word in Latin could stand for several words in English. My rather confused notion that languages should have a one-to-one vocabulary correspondence took a long time to break down. Long after this I retained a similar fallacious idea that Latin was easy because you didn't need to learn as many words as in English. It is an interesting commentary that despite this cramming technique I gained five credits and a distinction in the School Certificate examinations of the Northern Joint Matriculation Board.

University studies were tackled initially in much the same manner. My mind was relatively uncluttered with facts and I found most of the subjects quite new and exciting. Starting with many diverse Intermediate subjects I found psychology, philosophy and logic fascinating, new languages a challenge and history lectures a joy to listen to. My facility for absorbing facts mechanically helped me gain a first in mediaeval history, in an ancient language and, curiously, in philosophy, where remembering and recalling the intricate arguments of Plato, Schleiermacher and Kant in the final examinations must have stood me in good stead. My one dismal failure was in English, where mechanical learning could not be applied to understanding the works of Dickens, George Eliot and Shakespeare.

Yet it was psychology which captivated me as a subject, at that time taught with verve and compassion by Professor T. H. Pear. I was fortunate in listening to a lively provocative mind, in a department where psychology was still seen as relating to human beings rather than to animals. When I moved on to a theological degree I continued this interest, often cutting lectures in theology to attend courses in psychopathology and psychoanalysis in the medical school. My tutors warned me that such irresponsible behaviour could lead to failure in my degree, and it afforded me some grim satisfaction that I should contradict their prophecies. It was this wide knowledge of many branches of psychology, academic, clinical and educational, which provided me with the opportunity to visit America and shaped my professional future.

While my previous intellectual starvation diet gave me an insatiable appetite for lectures and reading, my real education took place in the hall of residence where I lived for several years. Here in studies, late into the night I would discuss and argue, often with an older and wiser student. The student house was also a forum for more constrained, orderly argument and I quickly mastered the necessary parliamentry procedures to become its Chairman for two years. As my social confidence grew I moved in university union circles, taking office in various political and religious societies. I was frequently dogmatic and insufferable in private matters, simply because I would not take custom, seniority in years or anything other than a demonstrably rational argument as the basis for accepting a point of view. But because I found student organizations important I learned to moderate this verbal aggression for social purposes. This private and public discussion with fellow students served in the place of tutorials, a rare experience in a Redbrick university in those days.

It soon became evident to me that I was growing away from my home, despite the fact that I was militantly working-class and politically active in left-wing politics. My time at home made me increasingly irritable since no one seemed to perceive why I wanted to read. When I attempted discussion my open questioning of every convention was simply not understood as an exploration of ideas, but was received by my mother with shocked outrage. The small talk, the three times weekly visits to the local Odeon (there were hearing aids for my mother), the evenings spent card playing were a crushing bore to me and there was no quiet place to read in the house, other than going to my unheated bedroom. Mercifully, I had to earn money in the vacations to pay my way in term time, so it was with mutual relief that I left home and became a mountain guide on most vacations in the English Lake District, Wales and Scotland. This widening gap between my mother and myself was, and still is, a source of guilt to me, for in those years she was frequently ill and, although I did not know it, slowly dying of bronchial disease. Yet being at home was like a slow death to me and leaving home felt like moving into a free world of light and rationality.

Perhaps I owed my social salvation to the fact that I spent my immediate post-graduate years in America on a fellowship. I discovered there that my odd social background was not in fact odd, but by American standards, quite normal. There were plenty of students working their way through college, many from more difficult beginnings than myself. My restless dissatisfactions found creative expression in research and writing and it was in Chicago that I first felt that education was more than the assimilation of facts but the capacity to enquire, think and behave independently.

Looking back at the power which impelled me forward, after so late a beginning, it seems to me to be due to many things, not least the happy accident of meeting stimulating people at the time when I was most ripe to receive their ideas. My motives in pressing forward were partly religious, partly political, partly idealistic in that I intuitively saw that if I wanted to contribute anything education held the key. I had no real idea what higher education meant, nor what it demanded, but once immersed in its processes it provided an intoxication of ideas and the excitement of exploring new areas of knowledge. Despite early retardation, a poor environment and disturbed family circumstances I somehow survived, my earlier deprivations creating an emotional and intellectual hunger, which drove me forward.

VI

RICHARD HOGGART[1]

*Professor of English and Director of the Centre for
Contemporary Cultural Studies, University of Birmingham*

I was born just North of the centre of Leeds, in a district called
Chapeltown, which seems to have become a lower-middle class
suburb but at that time contained the remnants of a village.
It was a village that had been enveloped in, I suppose, the late-
nineteenth century. As you came off the main road you dropped
down a wideish lane, and on the right were a few stone-built
houses and cottages and courts. Ours was No. 48, Potternewton
Lane, in a little court to itself. Cramped in the corner was this
old-fashioned house, which may have been a farm labourer's
house at one time.

The area was half surrounded by working-class terrace
houses of the slightly better late-nineteenth-century kind.
Immediately in front of us there was a field and I remember
as a boy (I must have been about five) seeing a cow calve in
this field. That was only about a mile and a half to two miles
from the centre of Leeds. I went back a few years ago and,
of course, the field doesn't exist; it's been obliterated by a lot of
'semis'.

The house itself had a living-room and, at the back of it, a
scullery with a single cold-tap. The stairs rose out of the living-
room and that had a big old-fashioned range. There was a room
over the living-room and, if I remember correctly, a small room
over the scullery. That's where my mother and the three of us
lived. There was an outside lavatory which I think was an
earth closet. It was funny, near the middle of a city full of

[1] Transcribed from a recorded conversation with the editor.

huddled working-class brick dwellings, to have this tiny court almost to ourselves. The story of the cow rather overstresses the rural quality. It was very much a pocket and we were very much part of Leeds. We were near one the big tram-depots, and I remember seeing the men picketing there during the 1926 strike. But still the flags in the yard and the stone of the house gave a kind of West Riding rural quality to it.

I don't really remember how the sleeping arrangements went, but I suspect that my sister slept with my mother and my brother with me. I was born in September 1918, my sister a couple of years later and my brother almost a couple of years before. My father had been a soldier; he must have died about 1921. From then on my mother was looking after us on her own. I can't really say I remember my father. Sometimes I think I do and then I wonder whether I'm remembering photographs of him. But my mother I remember fairly well. Most of the time she was tired and ill. We were living wholly on Public Assistance. I remember one relative who seemed well-to-do to us. She may have worked in Montague Burton's factory or one of the other big tailoring firms for about £2 a week. That seemed affluence. And I remember someone producing a small packet of mixed biscuits—before that, I had only seen them in shop-windows. If my mother wanted to cheer us up or get us over an awkward hump or keep us quiet for a while she would give us a half-slice of bread, with a bit of margarine and some tinned, condensed milk on it. It was cheap foreign condensed milk and had a special character of its own: the sugar they laced it with somehow hadn't melted and it had a gritty quality.

We children usually just wandered around the roads in Chapeltown or Potternewton. If we wanted to make something of an expedition we would go about a mile, across the main road, to a park. I imagine we were a fairly closed-in family. A widow and her three children—just managing on Public Assistance—were bound to be slightly separated from others.

My father was the next to eldest child of a family of ten, and his mother was one of the older ones of a family of nine or ten. She was born and brought up in Boston Spa, which is a few miles outside Leeds. It was rather a feudal place, a village with landowners and the remnants of a ruling gentry. My grand-

mother, my father's mother, was the daughter of a farm hand—
although I think probably a sort of foreman—and she married
her cousin, who was also of that village. He was from a big
family, too. Then they became part of a representative movement we all know about. I imagine their marriage was in the
early 1870s (she was born in the fifties). This young woman
with her husband came to Leeds or Sheffield first, drawn like so
many to the big industrial centres. He was a fairly talented man,
I gather, in that he had an inventive streak; and he moved
around more than a normal labourer would. Finally they
settled in Leeds.

We've got a family legend of a common kind—that he invented something (I think it was a way of picking up huge steel
sheets so that as they rose there was no danger of the clamp
giving way, dropping the sheets and killing men. His device
caused the clamp to tighten as the sheets rose higher and higher
and this, my older relatives used to say, is still used). The story
ends that he didn't get his dues for it, that he was paid a small
lump sum by the works and no royalties. Other stories suggest
that he was an independent-minded man. I've heard recently,
from an aunt who is now in her nineties, an account of how he
got the sack at Loughborough. He was working as a craftsman
in a big factory, making machines for boots and shoes. The
foreman handed back something he had made. He thought it
was good and that the foreman was insecure and only trying to
establish his authority. My grandfather is said to have stood
up and answered: 'Well, you can do it yourself', then thrown
it at the foreman's feet, demanded his cards and walked out.
So they were on the move again. My grandmother had her ten
children in several different parts of the country. Once in Leeds,
they settled in the big, industrial-barrack region of Hunslet,
and that is where—very much later—I come in. When we were
living in Potternewton, my mother would very occasionally
take us on the double tram-ride—from Potternewton into town,
then on to the Hunslet tram to see my grandmother. I don't
remember my grandfather at all, though you could say that his
spirit lived on in the house for years. Families like that had a
strong sense of the father's importance. 'My father always used
to say . . .' was a common opening remark.

My own father too seemed to have various jobs. I think he served in the Boer War, but in what capacity I don't know. On my own birth certificate he's shown as a house painter. But I imagine this is something he happened to be doing at the time I was born. For patches he was certainly in the Regular Army. But that, of course, was one of the things working men who couldn't settle, or simply couldn't find work, often did for a spell. Then he went to the First World War. I think he had a period in the Pay Corps. At one time he was a Sergeant, it may have been in the infantry. His army record must be all right, because I got a grant for clothing from the British Legion when I was a student at Leeds and they presumably looked up the records. The story is that he got Maltese fever in Malta, though again this may be one of those pieces of family folk-lore. You expected to send one of your family abroad to tramp around the Empire with the troops; you half expected him to pick up strange diseases. Again, some of my family say that if everybody had had their rights, we'd have had a pension for my father's Maltese fever. I think they tried, and the Government said it wasn't certain that his death was due to the fever. I gather there was a long-standing chest trouble. I have to 'watch my chest' and this may be a legacy. My father was probably in his middle-forties when he died. I don't think he married young. I'm told he met my mother in York when he was doing a spell of military service. His surviving sisters talk about him as though he was a man of great self-determination but with a certain kind of wildness.

As to my grandparents on my mother's side, I am even more vague. The story is that my mother was of a 'better class' family. I think that may be true so long as you realize the fine shadings you can have in that phrase 'better class'. She was certainly from Liverpool: my brother and I once went over for a week just after my mother died to stay with some of her relatives. They seemed to range from lower-middle to quite comfortable-middle class; and they didn't seem to feel upstarts. We stayed in an area which looked to us well-to-do. I think it was probably a respectable, lower-middle class, terrace region with bay-windowed houses, small gardens, and narrow halls. But to have a hall, with a bit of stained glass, was rather grand.

This was one of my mother's sisters, and she was very kind. She took us to see her daughter, who had married the Captain of a banana boat, and lived in a 'semi' in a comfortable modern part of Liverpool.

So my mother's family were not poor working-class. My relatives on the Hoggart side, when they mention my mother, say things like, 'Ah! She was a lady, was your mother.' They talk about her voice, and they say that once I began to lose my Leeds accent the intonations I kept were those of my mother. What she was doing in York I don't really know. I've heard it said that she went away from home because it was frustrating and that she decided to make her own way. The story is that when my father met her she was serving in the canteen of a soldiers' barracks or something like that. From his photographs, he seems to have been a well-set-up man with a thick moustache and, in those tight 1914 jackets, a strong-looking Tommy Sergeant sort of person. He was a good-sized man as well, bigger than I am. I don't know whether she was swept off her feet. She was a slim woman. I remember the long dark dresses that she used to wear, that swished, and those lace-up boots. I've got a sense of her way of talking, a way which wasn't Leeds working-class; but that may be something I've invented from hearing people describe it. I do remember one or two little incidents when her relatives asked my brother and me—they called us 'Addie's kids'—over for that week's holiday. All in all they were kind and anxious to give us a good time. But just once or twice I got the sense that we were the children of Addie who had stepped down in the world. I don't think they were conscious of making us feel that way; only, I remember little conversations I overheard. Children have ears the size of footballs, especially if they're looked after by strange adults.

But to come back to our house when my mother was alive. Hardly anything happened, as you can imagine, and a visitor was unusual. My mother used to draw her small amount of money and, under the system in those days, I think part of it was given in coupons which she had to spend at certain specified grocers' shops, such as the Maypole. This was money from the Board of Guardians, as they then were. She used to go down about once a week, I suppose to an office, to collect it, though people did occasionally appear from the Local Authority. Our food was about as basic as it could be: tinned cocoa and condensed milk at about threepence a tin. There were no luxuries. I think she had to be very shrewd to keep the boat steady and that she must have had great pride. She was always anxious not to be looked down upon. I've not ever heard that she earned any extra money; she was hardly well enough. She always had chest trouble and died of bronchitis.

For breakfast, we had a piece of bread and, if there was dripping, dripping and a cup of cocoa. The cocoa was cheap and gritty like the condensed milk; but it was a sensible thing to give us. I remember that, when we had meat, it was usually very cheap stew; but this, after all, is peasant fare all over Europe and is, in fact, very nourishing. Tea was usually bread and butter and there might possibly be a jar of cheap jam. We had a cup of cocoa at night. This seems the sort of diet that would have commended itself to those Quakers who are interested in the diet of the working-class, in that within its limits it provided a lot of nourishment. We never saw fish-and-chips or shop-prepared food of that kind. I have a photograph of myself round about that time and I did look healthy; in fact, I was chubby. I remember that I used to go to a shop next door—an old woman kept it—and she always called me 'Sonny Jim'. Of course, we were cheaply dressed; but we were 'neat and tidy and well cared for'. My mother used to get clothing cheques as well as food cheques, from the Board of Guardians. I remember once she dressed the two boys in those sailor suits which used to be so popular. That must have been at Whitsuntide, the annual occasion for children's new clothes. She was terribly proud of us and she was always ready to fight for her brood. She took us, in the sailor suits, to see my grandmother; and one of my aunts still remembers how on such occasions she used to sit with her back straight and want us to be admired. The day my sister had to have glasses, I remember my mother sitting and crying. All her pride and her sense of self-identity must have been bound up with her three kids.

We had no radio in the home, and if there were any books I never noticed them. There was a lot of children's chatter but not much conversation because hardly anybody ever came in. I suppose we chattered about school, but it was a closed world. My mother was certainly not an intellectual. It is very hard to see down this long tunnel; I imagine she would have seemed withdrawn to strangers, because she was rather grey and under-par much of the time, but fighting to keep a good face on things. I remember coming in one day and finding her lying on the clip-rug in front of the hearth. Her chest was really playing her up and she'd been coughing. I'm not sure if it was consumption, but it was at least bad bronchitis. We were frightened because we didn't know what it was. I suspect she was well on her way to her last illness. Then everything goes hazy, because children are like dumb animals when things like that happen. I suppose I saw my mother in her coffin; it was normal, but I can't remember. I do remember relatives converging from Hunslet and then, of course, from Liverpool, when she died. I suspect she was buried from my grandmother's home in Hunslet. This makes me think that she probably died in hospital but that arrangements were made for the coffin to be brought by the undertaker to my grandmother's, and that they just gave up our old house. It would revert to the landlord, I expect, and be let again for the usual few shillings a week. I don't remember the funeral itself but I remember the funeral day clearly. I remember the great crowd in my grandmother's because it brought together my father's sisters and brothers, the Hoggart group, and some from Liverpool.

Then I moved to my grandmother's in Hunslet. That area was mid- to late-nineteenth century, Industrial Revolution, cheap speculative housing for workers. There are areas like this all over the big industrial cities, especially from the Midlands upwards. It's just been knocked down, in these last two years. There was the centre of Leeds and you crossed the river, going South, and got into the heavy industrial area where the gasworks were, the railway sidings, the canals and the main arterials to London. We were off the right hand side, about one mile from the city centre. You came off the road and started walking up a slight incline and you were in row after row of symmetrical, brick, back-to-back houses with cobbled streets, corner shops and a little board school. As it happened—

there's always an oddity—at one point there was a Roman
Catholic school in the middle of it all, and just at the back of
this, between it and the cobbled street, they'd put a small row
of brick houses which they didn't make back-to-back because,
I suppose, they couldn't have back access to them. They were
through-houses with tiny open yards and then a wall to the
Catholic school playground. We were in one of those, the end
one. It was an advantage, having the end one, because it meant
that we had a side-yard which you could have even put a hand-
cart in, or if you had been a window cleaner you could have
kept your ladders there. The yard was 'L' shaped. Everybody
else had a bit of yard with old palings they'd made out of
orange-boxes, and one of them kept pigeons.

There were two lavatories in our yard; the left-hand one was
shared by us and the people next door. They were, when I
arrived, earth closets but were later made into cheap water
closets. The yard was in some sense common because the
'rubbish hole' was there, between the two lavatories. We had,
in the house itself, a living-room into which you walked straight
off the street, and behind that a scullery. I think we had a cellar
too. There were narrow stairs coming out of the living-room.
Upstairs, there was a front bedroom over the living-room and
a back bedroom over the scullery. But the thing that made
the house cost a shilling or one and sixpence a week more than
the other houses in that street, or that area, was that there was
an attic which went over both living-room and scullery. This,
of course, was spacious by comparison with any other room.
When she'd moved in there, my grandmother must have been
in what Rowntree calls one of the more prosperous phases of
working-class life; that is, with her children grown up and her
husband still working. They'd move to this house because they
felt able to pay the odd shilling and sixpence a week more. At
some date somebody had put a bath in the attic. This was
unusual. We had a screen made out of a large clothes-horse
which had been covered in left-over bits of wall paper. It was
put round the bath so that someone could have a bath when
somebody else was in bed. That was where I slept. If the neighbours had something special on—say, a daughter getting
married—they would ask whether she could have a bath.

We were broken up as a family that day at my mother's funeral in my grandmother's living-room. I remember the conversation about what should be done with us. I can remember someone saying that orphanages were very good nowadays, and that we'd probably be better looked after there than in any individual family. Of course, a child felt immediately threatened and isolated. But the majority wouldn't hear of this; all their traditions were against it. What they were feeling, I think, was that nothing could make up for 'belonging to somebody' rather than being part of a public institution. I was the only one who went to my grandmother. My sister went to a half-aunt in the next street. My brother went to Sheffield, to my grandmother's oldest daughter, the second of her children. She had eleven children of her own; and her husband was a railway waggon-driver. Sheffield was a long, long way from Leeds, about forty miles. I saw my sister fairly often, of course, in the next street. I went over to Sheffield to see my brother at odd intervals, perhaps once a year for a few days during the school holidays. He came over once or twice. I lived with my grandmother until she died, having gone to her when I was seven or eight years old. She died in January 1937, just after I had gone up to Leeds University.

There were six at my grandmother's; myself, a grand-daughter from Sheffield looking for work (this was during the slump), and three unmarried children of my grandmother, ranging in age from about 30 to 50 years.

I can't remember much about the schooling in Chapeltown, except that I enjoyed it. It was the nearest local school and had a stone plaque saying that this was a Board School built after the 1870 Act or something to that effect. I can't remember feeling that I was more intelligent than any of the others. At seven or eight, when I changed homes, I went to what they called Jack Lane Elementary School in Hunslet. I remember the shock of this South Leeds slum school, which again suggests that the Chapeltown area might not have been solidly, toughly, working-class. I remember being beaten by the inevitable bully, for 'talking posh' in Hunslet. Interesting, because I must have had a broad Leeds voice; but there would be just that edge to it which the Hunslet ear picked up and thought was up-staging them. I was on the whole unhappy at Jack Lane. There was one particular bully, who took it out of me viciously and gave me my first taste of anti-Semitism, which is quite a strong strain in some areas of working-class life. I'm not a Jew, but he decided for some reason to say I was. I think the basic reason was that he looked like a Jew himself and was ashamed of it. So he would come up and get me against a wall and say, 'Sheeny,' and hit me.

It was a school for boys only and the teachers had to be tough. Or rough. I can remember a master I had for a year there who was a shocker. He finally had to flee the country to escape some sort of charge. It was said that for one thing he was homosexual and for another that he had defaulted with the savings of the local football club, and that the police had finally closed in on both counts. He disliked me because I didn't respond to his emotional blackmail. One day he sang in class a sentimental Irish song about 'Mother' until gradually—and it was what he was after—he had almost every boy in tears. When he saw I wasn't crying he turned on me and deliberately tried to disturb me by stirring memories of my own mother. There were certainly one or two class teachers there who helped, but I can't clearly remember them. It's a pity, but one can easily forget the steady good work some teachers put in, even though they never actually fire your imagination. The teacher I remember best at that school was the headmaster, who decided early on that I was bright. He had been to a training college, gone pupil teaching and then come to Hunslet and saw himself as in some way helping to civilize it. He could be as tough as anyone; yet he had the will and patience, if he saw some talent in a boy, to help it along. Without being soft, he helped me a lot. I never really knew this till later; it's remarkable how much you *don't* notice when you're a child (and how much you *do* notice, in other ways). I remember that when I had pneumonia and nearly died—I was about nine or ten years old—the headmaster came to the house to see me, which is unusual. I don't suggest I saw a great deal of him, but I knew he was in the background.

The morning I took the scholarship exam, I walked to Cockburn High School, which is a local L.E.A. 1902 grammar-school, to sit the papers. As far as I know, nobody before had gone in for it from our school, though there may have been another one or two who went with me. Incidentally, I think it would do some of us good if we could go back to those slum schools and see how inadequate and ill-equipped much of the teaching was thirty or forty years ago. So many teachers were sweating it out, ill-paid; they hadn't been well-trained themselves or had any refresher training. I'm sure it's better than that now in most schools, a good deal better. I was ill-prepared for the exam and, of course, failed it. But when you talk to people around my age about that exam you discover that many who are now reasonably successful failed to pass.

I was told that my headmaster then went down to the local education office and said to them, 'Look at this boy's essay; there's some talent here,' and they decided to give me a place at Cockburn. I don't know whether they did actually re-read the essay. But I went to Cockburn. Cockburn was lavatory-tiled up to elbow height inside, a brick cube outside. There were several masters and mistresses—it was co-ed—who had a sense of 'mission' of one kind or another. There was a Latin master who was tough and effective; his sights were set on getting good School Certificates. He had a house nearby, in the Dewsbury Road area, and lived for his work. He would smile on all those boys who worked hard because he thought you could achieve anything by work. He would be very severe on others. I was hard-working so he was always helpful, and he taught me a lot about keeping your head down and going at it. There was a very nice English master—I see now, rather sentimental but warm and friendly. There was a good French mistress too who tried to see through to the sort of person you might become. Cockburn is a curious, interesting school. It's had a succession of quite well-known or successful alumni by now; I can think of three professors from the tiny Arts Sixth in my time alone. But, then, there'd been a lot of sifting.

By the time you'd gone through all the hoops to get to Cockburn you were either very good indeed, or you had enormous staying-power or self-preservation or luck. You had been brought up in one of these streets, and in a bookless home— this was true of almost every boy or girl in that area, especially on the Hunslet side. The Dewsbury Road side, which the school also drew upon, was slightly 'posher'. To have been at one of these elementary schools, to have sat the scholarship exam when the number of places, compared with those today, was tiny and to have got a place—all this was much harder than it is today. I sometimes have an imaginary aerial picture of a typical morning, at the time I started at Cockburn—of one door opening and a boy coming out with a new Cockburn cap, one boy contributed from a big range of streets and probably being called at by the other boys as he went; then another one from another street and so on. Then they began to make their friendships from a wider range around.

The headmaster of Cockburn in my time, who didn't stay there long, was an odd character. He had been a master at Dulwich College. He left Cockburn to go into an Anglican monastery. He came to Cockburn because he wanted to try his hand at this type of school. He was a Southerner with a markedly middle-class southern voice. It's said that he was very forgetful and one year forgot to send off the completed matriculation papers. Many of the teachers seem to have thought him a poorish headmaster. But he wasn't for me. I'd never met anyone like him before. I remember once, when I was in the Upper Fifth, for some reason he marked or looked at a set of essays. I had written one on Hardy and had begun it, 'Thomas Hardy was a truly cultured man. . . .' He stopped me a day or two later, swung against the door of his study, and said, 'What is "a truly cultured man", Hoggart?' I was baffled. I thought he was playing me up, because if our headmaster didn't know what a truly cultured man was, if the phrase wasn't absolutely cast-iron, where were we? And he said, 'Am I one? I don't think so. I don't feel myself "truly cultured".' This was my first sight of a mind speculating, of thought as something disinterested and free-playing, with yourself outside it. I usually thought of a master as somebody who said, 'This is what the such-and-such a verb is, or this is what happened in 1762, and you have to learn it.' That's one key person and later I had the good luck to be one of Bonamy Dobrée's students in the English Department at Leeds University. I have written about that elsewhere. One of the things both my headmaster and professor did

101

for me, and perhaps this is where my interest in cultural change starts, was to give me a feeling for cultural comparisons, between the cultures of the North and South in England, and between different social classes. They also helped me to get used to arguing and disagreeing, *without taking it personally*.

My grandmother was pleased and proud that I'd got to grammar-school, and she helped to make it easier to do homework, and in lots of other ways. There was still a sense in her of the old respect for learning. She used to tell me with great pride that 'poet Longfellow' and 'painter Hogarth' were both members of our family, and I think she was right. She read quite difficult books, which was unusual in a woman of her age and background. There were a handful of books in the house, because an uncle there also had some literary interest—one of her sons, the youngest. And we had the usual two or three volumes of Dickens given away by newspapers, a few woman's novelettes, of the sort that were presented at Chapel Anniversaries, but no great range. If there was a Bible it was never on show. I suspect there was one, but by and large there was little of the Bunyan-and-the-Bible tradition in the home. My grandmother was officially Church of England, but in an unexpectant, countrified way; she didn't make much of it. Certainly she had imagination and a latent capacity for intellectual excitement. I did my homework on the end of the table; obviously, there could be no heating in a bedroom. She always reminded me to do my homework and wouldn't let me go out to play till it was done. She would worry a bit if there was too much noise and say, 'The lad's got to get on.' It was recognized that it had to be done, but there were sharp limits to what they could physically make arrangements for. There were also what you might call imaginative limits, in that it would have been expecting too much of them to get everybody to hush up because I was doing my homework. There was no radio until quite late in the twenties or early thirties, when we could afford it.

I don't remember consciously getting the idea of going forward to higher education. I did what I was told to do, one step after the other. I didn't have a perspective, a vision of a goal. I enjoyed doing the work. I was in some ways timid and though

I had a kind of quirky, urgent quality, I usually just went on.
But I suppose I wouldn't have gone on if I hadn't enjoyed it
at bottom. I did my four years to matriculation, during which
time I had one nervous breakdown. That may have been a way
of paying off a lot of strains that had been considerable before
then; I've been able at least just to cope with my worst situations since. Then I took a very good matric. I hadn't even
thought of a job, though I suppose I would have simply gone
into town to a Labour Exchange or looked in the local paper.
The headmaster put at the bottom of his report, 'Should think
of professional life.' My grandmother didn't know quite what
to make of that. She had an idea what professions were, but
she didn't know exactly what it meant. So she asked the Board
of Guardians' visitor, a lady called Miss Jubb who used to come
from the Leeds Authority every so often and was very helpful
and rather proud of me, because she didn't have many scholarship boys on her list. She said, 'It means that he could well
become, say, a doctor.' Then she said, 'Wait and see.' If I've
got my figures right, up to then the Guardians were paying seven
shillings and sixpence a week for me, all in, and they increased
it for my sixth-form work to about fifteen shillings; and on this
my grandmother felt she could go ahead, and was glad to do so.

So I worked for Higher School Certificate and after that there
was talk of university, but there was never any suggestion of
going to Oxbridge. The daughter of one of the senior masters
went, I remember, to Oxford, but she'd had a special year's
training. I didn't think much about making a choice of any
particular university. The word seemed to get round that you
went to Leeds University—instead of to a training college—
if you did very well. I think the figure was then twenty Senior
City scholarships; that is, twenty university scholarships from
the Leeds L.E.A., every year, for the whole city of nearly half-
a-million people. I don't remember being interviewed in advance
at the University. I got a letter saying what I'd done in Higher
School Certificate and it was good; and a letter saying I had been
accepted by the English Department at Leeds University. I
knew I wanted to do English and I imagine that my English
master said, 'You want to do English, don't you?' and I said,
'Yes,' and it went down on a form somewhere.

I was always a keen reader. I obviously had a respectable sort of mind, one that *would* have passed the eleven-plus scholarship exam with better training. For instance, I had the usual interest in working out abstract patterns. I got a Grade I at School Certificate in Maths, in spite of having failed Maths at eleven, so there was some ability there. As for imaginative excitement, the first real instance I remember was when I was standing one day—I must have been about eleven at the time— in Hunslet Public Library. I picked up a complete Swinburne, read a lot of it and wanted to cry. That was the moment I first consciously felt the excitement of poetry. I can never scoff at Swinburne, though his faults are obvious, because he was making me respond to the wonder of words in their own right. But basically one went on, at Cockburn, doing the job. The literature work I loved, and became, as boys like me so often do, very mannered in my writing, mannered and poetic. The masters always said, 'You're too elaborate.' It takes a long time to work out.

On going up to university I was in a mixed frame of mind. I was interested and eager; but I didn't go up feeling that this was to be the most wonderful period of my life. I knew I hadn't enough money to do anything very special. In my first year, when I'd paid for everything, I had left over for pocket money each week—that is to pay for any books, fares, smoking, tooth-paste and soap, fish-and-chips, cinemas and so on—one shilling and sixpence; and you couldn't cut a dash on that even in the thirties. I was not isolated because of this, since there were several others in that position. On the other hand, we felt a bit sniffy about students who took their pressed-cardboard attaché cases to the university each day from nine to five, and seemed to have settled for a subfusc routine. We had to create our own style on the cheap, so to speak. What pleased me about university life was, again, meeting people who were intellectually interested, who liked ideas and their relations to experience. Without that I would have gone on and done the work expected of me, but at the same time I would have felt detached from it. I could always hang from the chandelier with my *alter ego*. I think one of my basic qualities, and I sus-pect it comes partly from the whole working-class tradition, is a kind of dissident, ironic, micky-taking quality. I can remember how even at twelve or thirteen one side of me was very impressed by the grammar-school masters, and I thought they lived lives of great comfort and luxury. But I also saw the long vista of what is often a kind of safe dreariness, and didn't like that at all.

Summing-up, I suppose there were several major turning-points in my childhood. The first was the move to my grandmother's home. Then, clearly, there was the scholarship exam at eleven. In terms of personalities: my grandmother, the headmaster of the elementary school, the headmaster of the secondary school and Bonamy Dobrée. Put another way, the changes from that enclosed life with my mother in Potternewton into the big South Leeds slum school. Then there was grammar-school, and entry into the sixth form; and the various moments of imaginative awakening, such as finding Swinburne's poems, and the discussion of essays by the headmaster. One of the strange things is how late it all seems to have been in my case.

I can recognize some characteristics, today, which I suppose are due to those experiences; though it's difficult to be sure. I often feel insecure and anxious to justify myself. I always feel guilty if I haven't 'done my homework', so to speak. I find it hard to relax sufficiently. Perhaps some of this is due to being an orphan, and changing homes. One of the obvious results of going to grammar-school was that it gave you another world to live in, a different world from that of the streets of Hunslet. It had advantages, but I still sometimes feel I am working out this isolation. I react too quickly to hints that I am being cut out, rejected. On the credit side is the non-conformity and dissidence I've mentioned, a capacity, now and again, to say 'come off it'; and an ability to go on going on.

VII

DENNIS MARSDEN

Sociology Research Officer, University of Essex

In 1951 at the age of eighteen I was the first of my family ever to go to Cambridge. Subsequently, Brian Jackson and I traced 88 ex-grammar-school pupils of about our age, who like us had come from working-class homes in Huddersfield. We asked them and their parents to describe their education and changing family relationships, and we wrote a book about these experiences called *Education and the Working Class*. The story of my own education repeats some of the main themes of the book, perhaps linking and highlighting them in a slightly unusual way. However, in the present volume of essays I think it's worth making the case again. The working-class child who gets through the education system by the conventional grammar-school route is frequently the subject of unusual forces and circumstances. And he may become a puzzled and insecure adult.

My aunts found *A Taste of Honey* appallingly immoral, *Saturday Night and Sunday Morning* remote but more recogizable. They belonged to a respectable, even Victorian, family of a type which tends to be overlooked in these times of Hoggart and Sillitoe. My father would recall how, when he was a child, on Sunday they were never allowed to sing a comic song or tell a joke, and how he himself had been brought in and made to stand at the cellar head for two hours because he had called somebody a devil. On Sunday evenings they would assemble for singing at the piano. Propriety of behaviour and thrift, with both money and feeling, were the roots of their respectability; keeping up appearances, keeping up one's standard of living, looking after one's money, keeping a tight rein on emotion. Deferential, upward-looking and prim, the family had initially at least a strong belief in the virtues and rewards of hard work, and a powerful sense of guilt and personal salvation. Below them, all around, was a rough working-class whose downfall was drink, a menace to both morals and pocket.

The seeds of respectability were there in my grandfather's day. He was a gas-meter inspector, not a great job, but one with some status and security. My father, his twin brother and five sisters were all born in a village suburb of Huddersfield, and until comparatively late in life never moved out of a radius of half a mile of one another. They nearly all worked in the mills as menders, spinners or weavers, but they eventually achieved minor supervisory posts, or met and married through their religion thrifty men who bought their own houses and usually other houses besides. Yet they were staunch Labour supporters, wavering only very little towards the edges of an old-fashioned Liberalism. If they did in any way identify with a higher class it was not the body of local burgesses or the small mill-owners and tradesmen with whom they had to do each day, but some remote professional or even higher class whom they never saw. They were nonconformist by tradition, although in fact more of them were church members than chapel. My aunts lived a rich organizational life centred on the church and Mothers Union, and through this they had a wide range of contacts. Sometimes they met socially their children's teachers, even head-teachers. There were, however, limits strictly set as to how much and in what way one could participate without attracting a charge of social climbing.

My father had a small, shy talent which was crushed by the circumstances of his upbringing and working life. He was a brainy boy, and recalled often with wry pride that he used to get nine out of nine on his school reports, three for reading, three for writing, and three for arithmetic. More than once an essay of his on 'A Loaf of Bread' or 'The Adventures of a Penny' had been so successful that he was taken into the upper school to have it read out. Unfortunately, when my father was only five his father died, and left my grandmother to bring up a large family as best she could. There was no possibility of my father sitting the scholarship, even though his older sisters must have been working by then. At thirteen my grandmother took him to a local mill and asked them to set him on: 'He's a poor fatherless lad, and Ah want to do t'best Ah can for him'. The best they could do was five shillings a week, sweeping up, fetching fish-and-chips for the older men who could afford them, and doing all the most boring jobs in the mill, such as reaching in, hooking threads over the end of a tool which someone pushed through the comb in a loom. As the experience came across to us children in my father's description the parallel was with the blacking factory days of Charles Dickens (in *David Copperfield* which incidentally, along with *Martin Chuzzlewit*, my father won for a Sunday-School prize). The acute consciousness of a wasted life, the bruising and blunting of a shy personality by the rough world of the mill, became the more unbearable to my father as he never got away from that world or even that particular mill. Not altogether joking, he would say for the shocked amusement of the rest of the family, 'If Ah'd known then what Ah know now, Ah'd have thrown meself in t'cut' (canal).

A tougher, more resilient, more adventurous man might have risen above this. He did try to break out. As a young child I recall his neat drawings of loom gears and shuttle mechanisms from his Tech. classes. He also learned cloth designing. But the depression further handicapped him when, with a young family, he was prevented from changing his job from the small mill where he worked to a larger place with more opportunity for his skills. As it was, his efforts merely resulted in his being given still more odd jobs to do without him attaining any one outstanding skill. Before I went to grammar-school these Tech. classes stopped, as in the evenings a more than physical weariness would overtake him. I chiefly remember him spasmodically reading, dropping into a doze, waking to listen to the Home Service. In his middle forties, he looked desperately round for an escape and contemplated a panic emigration, to Cumberland, to Devon, or to Norwich. He was offered a partnership in a firm, but he hesitated too long. After that his working life was a slow decline, made bitter-sweet by our success at grammar-school.

My friends who met him in later years would have found it difficult to imagine his earlier reputation as something of a deep freethinker. The shelf at home still holds an Esperanto dictionary. He had once given a paper on Malthus to the chapel Young Men's group, and for a time he was a chapel trustee. He was a member of the committee of a Refugee Relief organization, and also of a Friendly Society. Yet, ironically, as he saw his children enter (as he thought) a less socially-trammelled world by means of education, his own confidence ebbed and his sense of imprisonment grew.

He still remained, in a dulling routine, surprisingly literate. He read Hardy, Conrad, Galsworthy, Jane Austen, Dickens, the Brontës, and a host of others. When we went to school he found a limited delight in poetry, from *Palgrave's Golden Treasury* and a curious volume called *1001 Gems of English Verse*. He admired particularly the famous bits from Shakespeare, for their high diction and, as he said, deep thought. Regularly we all went to the library, and if what my mother read was usually something romantic, at least it was in a library book, so the joys of a good read were early and constantly impressed on us by example. This literacy ran through the rest of the family. My father's eldest sister could occasionally win national crossword puzzles, and wrote letters to the papers.

My father and mother had met through chapel, my mother having come down from Cumberland into service in the house of a big mill-owning family. The widows and spinsters of the house had strong financial and spiritual links with the local chapel, and all the servants had to attend service there three times on a Sunday. After chapel, suitably chaperoned by a plain friend, my mother and father would walk out. Typically their courtship was long and cautious. My father was thirty-two when they married, by which time they had amassed enough capital to buy a house, and my mother had delivered an ultimatum that she could stand the big house no longer. Her family come little into the story of my education. Having been thus severed from her source of growth, she lived out her life very intensely through us children. Our month-long visits to Cumberland once a year were like a foreign adventure into a more fee and easy world of council-house dwellers and hard drinkers. For my mother's relatives were in some ways the warm embodiment of that harsh, indigent image which the Marsdens had made of the rough working-class.

To a child at the younger end of the Marsden family, life was cosy and protected. True, there were the occasional disappointments—a tricycle, when what one really wanted was a proper bicycle with a chain—but we were well fed and reasonably dressed. We were too young to know when my father's wage was unforgettably (and unforgivably) cut from three guineas to three pounds a week. I and my brother ate our meals at table with our parents, beneath a picture entitled, I think, *The Puritan's Dilemma*, showing a man in a tall hat torn between bread and red wine offered by two serving women. On Sunday afternoons we walked through the countryside or looked at Victoriana in the local museum after Sunday School. Sunday School calls up memories of the dreaded anniversary, sententious addresses by fat ladies and gentlemen; chapel bazaars with bran-tubs, and concerts where men sang comic songs and ladies sang excerpts from Handel. Our whole family had a tightly reciprocal visiting pattern. There would be formal teas between different aunts and uncles and children, with an inflexible menu of salad, tinned fruit and cream, and cakes, cake-baking carrying much status. Parties at birthdays and Christmas times had games such as 'King William' at first, but later we had brain-twisters, jumbled words, 'Country, county, town . . .' spelling bees. Then the newly-fledged grammar-school pupil could shine, and the younger hopefuls polish their verbal skills. There was no conscious preparation in all this, but how perfectly these games must have dovetailed with the scholarship exam.

Although we were a reading family, our bed-time story would be perhaps a reminiscence of naughty Harry Appleyard climbing out of the back window when the police came to get him for pinching apples, or some other story of misdoings calculated to thrill a well-protected child. In bed and in the talk at family parties the picture of family history and myth was built up. One ancestor was Black Alf, a stern lay preacher. Another was a real aristocrat: like many other families we should have been riding in our coaches, for according to the story my great grandmother was the beautiful but wayward daughter at a large house and she had eloped with a Marsden gardener. All day long she would sit in her gown and never do a hand's turn, for she knew nothing of housework.

I used to wonder if this was why my eldest aunt spoke with what we all considered a neutral English; she spoke 'nicely' and so did her children, somehow the way people in a state of nature would talk. But possibly it was a spell of some years as a children's nurse which had left their mark in deference and aspiration. At the other end of the speech scale was my father's brother, a rough diamond who spoke more nearly standard Huddersfield-workman than anyone else in the family. He learned comic monologues about Albert Ramsbottom and Pendleby Pit. At family parties there was a curious tension between him and the prim young high-school girls who wanted to recite 'Bunches of Grapes', by Walter de la Mare.

My uncle's comic role, was paralleled in the family's treatment of those members of the rough working-class with whom they had face-to-face relationships. We laughed with a slight shock at their apparent fecklessness, violence or the directness which to us bordered on rudeness. A Barnsley branch of the family were miners, mighty drinkers and fighters, and one popular story was how it took six policemen to get Great Uncle Ratcliff to jail. Black beer shandy was the nearest we came to real beer at our family parties.

One uncle was a member of the Huddersfield Choral Society, and every year he could get tickets for several relatives to hear a performance of 'The Messiah'. So it was *our* 'Messiah', and we felt at such times that the eyes of the musical world were on our Huddersfield. Handel led the younger members of the family into appreciation of other music, although our elders remained curiously frozen to this one work. The Brontës were a literary counterpart of our musical stake in high culture. Most of the family had probably read *Wuthering Heights* or *Jane Eyre*; but somehow this was irrelevant. To go and have tea at Haworth village seemed in itself a literary experience, all of a piece with hearing Wilfred Pickles read 'Wee bonny brid' on the Home Service. Imperceptibly this culture fused, via Yorkshire, with the Yorkshire branch of Royalty at Harewood.

Now out of all these adults in my father's generation, only one had any secondary education and that was at Central School. Yet out of the children who made up my generation only one failed to pass the scholarship, and she was paid for to go to commercial school. The rest went mostly to grammar-schools, although three of the boys ten or fifteen years older than me went to technical school on the advice of middle-class church acquaintances. The eldest boy of all, who went to grammar-school, later gained an external degree and quickly rose to become a senior Civil Servant. One of the boys who went to technical school eventually became a teacher through financial support from his parents. Later, another boy in the family was paid for, initially, at university after he had made the double mistake of leaving grammar-school at sixteen and studying the wrong subject at the Tech. for two years; he became a doctor. Three of his four sisters became nurses: one of the nurses is now Health Visitor in charge of a region; another sister married a doctor. The fourth sister married a high-grade Civil Servant. Two other girls in the family became teachers, and married teachers. A girl history graduate became a regional Child Care officer. My brother after graduating has become an electronics engineer. I was next to the youngest in this generation and I reached Cambridge.

Looked at in another way, five out of the fifteen children gained degrees, another three reached training college, and nearly all the remaining girls took nursing courses to an advanced level. In the *next* generation some children are already at public and direct-grant schools; others may go. One of my cousins tried to send a boy to Eton!

My father didn't exactly choose our primary school, but when upon marriage he bought a house in a very mixed area he invested his money better than he knew. We were in the catchment area of a most 'successful' school. The district shaded rapidly from back-to-back houses (with outside toilets, no bath, and a cellar-head kitchen), to suburban 'semis', and again to corporation houses. We had an inside toilet and bath in our small terrace house, but about half my friends had no such facilities. In our front street lived both our first infants teacher and the man who was to become our last sixth-form master. Children born near the centre of town by the gasworks thought our district decidedly 'posh'. Yet our house cost only £500 when new.

The local school was so successful because it crammed its pupils. One of my earliest recollections of lessons is kneeling at a bench when I was six or seven with the panicky consciousness that I was required to write a story. Perhaps I read too much into the incident, or gave the wrong slant. It is vivid for me because it catches the pattern of my later education, when like over-cultivated land too much production was extorted from me for the amount of food given to the vital centres.

At this time my mother's employers were on visiting terms with the heads of the grammar-schools which my cousins attended. But this visiting was very different from ours, for although the employers were kind and took a strong interest in me right up to university, tea at the big house was an awesome occasion and we felt poor relations. What impelled me towards grammar-school was not this glimpse of genteel life nor any concrete ambition for the future. It was fear of the bigger working-class boys at the elementary school. Juniors had to pass through the 'Big Boys' department during the vital two years before the scholarship examinations, and here discipline was much tougher and more brutal. Totally enveloping those big boys was an air of violence largely of the teachers' making, for the school's grinding routine of testing had to be imposed with the cane and the fist. At eight, boys and girls were segregated; and I did not again have an easy relationship with a girl until I was twenty. Arithmetic and spelling tests absorbed the attention formerly held by crushes. Though I *knew* my immersion in this world was to be only temporary—my brother having just passed for grammar-school—it was traumatic. I tried to stay away from school. Each week we were rearranged according to test results, and I sat always in the top three, but no one could avoid the wholesale caning of the last year. When the scholarship came it was an enjoyable release.

My father had time off work to take me to the grammar-school. Yet in this proud moment I had a sensation which has come to me again twice in my education. More than sheer loneliness, I knew what a mountaineer feels on an exposed climb. My three best friends had all gone to other schools. Equally promising with me, Jimmy was an orphan so he went automatically to the technical school (a fact, by the way, that did much to fix the knowledge of that school's lowly position in our minds). Malcolm's mother wanted him out working, so he also went to that school. Bobby passed on a different list from me and went to the third-choice grammar-school. He became a mill worker. I have scarcely had any contact with him since.

After a while, I regained a nervous equilibrium, though few could ever have been really comfortable in that grammar-school. Nobody caned me. They didn't need to, for the demands of work kept us on edge, particularly the top five or so. We were trained on a four-year fast course by a system of fortnightly marks and testing in every subject. Good work was rewarded by a half-day holiday. Then—poor caged birds that we were—we experienced infinite loneliness at being out of lessons for an hour or two.

Those first years at grammar-school must have been times of hardship for my parents. They had to buy books at that time in addition to the uniform and games equipment. My mother went back to work, to pay for these things as it appeared to me: in moments of stress later she would say, 'I should have made you leave.' But there never seemed any alternative to grammar-school. Difficulties in no way weakened our resolve, though they did deepen my sense of obligation. My repayment was to sit ever longer over my homework (with the wireless very firmly off), while the tight little circle of dozing father and ironing mother grew tighter, and so did the pressure for success.

After the first few months my father couldn't help me with school work. But my brother close ahead of me at school became a substitute middle-class parent and the sort of guide he badly needed himself at several stages of his school life. As the first child in an unfamiliar situation he seems to have escaped some of the pressures which bore on me. His strong

114

scientific curiosity got him through school, but he was less amenable to bullying in subjects which didn't interest him. Also he had trouble with languages, where more outside help would have been useful. About the third year he slipped from a precarious position in the A stream to the B's. This was obviously a humane action on the school's part; and subsequently my brother was overlooked in the grooming for Oxbridge and quite easily achieved his limited objective of a scholarship to Leeds. But to my parents the move downstream was an occasion for tears, recriminations and bad temper, a very powerful object lesson for me had any been needed. My brother had to help me with languages, for early on I took a Latin test having no conception of vocabulary, number, declension, case, gender or conjugation, and I got nought out of ten. That same evening my brother was forced by my parents to persevere with me until I had a working basis for learning the subject. I could never have asked the teacher. Possibly this help, as much as anything else, was crucial in keeping me in the running for Cambridge.

The art-mistress noted that I wouldn't use my imagination; but the whole school, the whole town and region, were geared to the sciences and technology. Most teachers lacked the will and technique to tap the inner lives of their pupils. In the A stream we dropped art very early; but the C stream continued with it, and this impressed upon us that such subjects were frills. I became a rote learner, and the few subjects demanding insight or personal vision came to appear unpredictable. Like slinging mud repeatedly at a brick wall in the hope that some of it would stick, I read *David Copperfield* five times all through for School Certificate. Then I felt vaguely cheated when English Literature and History were the two subjects in which I failed to get distinctions in that examination.

I had distinctions in all my science subjects. My brother was already reading science. The school's senior teachers and sixth-form masters (who, incidentally, lived within a stone's-throw of my home) were a chemist and a mathematician. I felt that arts subjects led merely to teaching. Five out of the top six boys in the A stream, including my two best friends, took science and maths. in the sixth form. So although I had no deep interest or involvement, as opposed to dexterity, in science it seemed the only possible choice of course.

I was forced to recognize the weakness in my position early in the sixth form during a mathematics lesson. The new teacher began by telling us that we were together on a different footing from boys lower down the school. We were here as students, not schoolboys. We were here because we wanted to learn. In that instant my path visibly narrowed. I looked round and noted how very *few* of us there were. I realized that I was there for many reasons, not least among them sheer inertia, obligation to my parents (and to teachers as the most successful boy of that year), and fear of leaving school. But a real desire to learn mathematics and science just was not among them. I found the work possible, but more and more difficult as I got further up the school.

Again I recovered, but the heights now seemed more vertiginous. I became conscious of my accent for the first time. I had no friends other than those I saw in class each day. And here the field of friendship was limited by a sort of jealous competition for the attention of masters and for the reassurance of academic superiority. (Many years later when my chief rival—making *his* escape from a narrow education—was killed in a climbing accident in the Himalayas, I was shocked to discover a sense of relief.) At first my mind had not been fixed on University. In spite of that grammar-school was always a state of waiting, almost of suspended animation, a kind of monastic novitiate. Only one of my close friends had any sort of relationship with girls. For the rest of us sex was confined to fantasy or lone visits to American musicals, which involved me very painfully at times. My brother's demotion was attributed by my parents and the school to his youth club. And relationships with girls were officially frowned upon apart from the carefully organized debates and inter-denominational sixth-form conferences. In our case, discouragement was hardly necessary. I was emotionally frozen, and sex came to have two aspects for me. It was a danger to academic work. And more than that it was lower-class. The friend who knew girls lived on a notorious council estate, and central-school boys whom I met at the town swimming-club also had girl friends. They seemed more confident and complete; yet all the time I felt that I was Grammar-School and my day would come. I joined no societies at school apart from the music club, and went on no school trips. I excelled only in the highly individualistic and very lonely sport of competitive swimming, where my approach was curiously similar to that of school work. Against the odds—I feel rather as a long shot which didn't come off—I was made a house captain. But I developed semi-psychological ailments which kept me away from school for the odd morning and precluded my entering for athletic sports or attending house-practices. As far as that side of school went I had a slipping clutch. When my Cambridge reference from the headmaster described me as a loyal member of the school, I felt peculiarly depressed. On reading the phrase I discovered that I actively didn't want to appear in that light.

As my life itself was held in abeyance during the sixth-form, so expectations of university built up. It slowly became clear that Oxford and Cambridge were what that school was about. I began to understand the message on the honours board in the gym, the achievements of Oxford and Cambridge scholarship winners which we read every day of our school lives as we waited in assembly. My father treasured up a remark, culled from one of the parent-teacher evenings which he always attended, that I 'should try for the highest honours'. 'You show 'em, Dennis lad,' he would say to me, now that we realized what those honours were. He would frequently come to look at me almost proprietorially as I worked (now in the front-room). This was a family effort, yet the divide between us was growing. My father began to make jokes about taking me for a walk to get to know me better. He must have sensed my lack of enthusiasm for the work which must follow my studies. Beyond University I couldn't see, indeed dared not and felt it unnecessary to look. One had to give an answer and mine was that I was going into industry. This seemed to satisfy inquirers, and in a grimly final way satisfied me. It also chilled my spirits, conjuring up a picture of the local chemical works by the dirty river on a wet day.

When I first went up to Cambridge for the scholarship examinations, the sheer isolation defeated me. I was quite alone from my school in a very old room in Peterhouse. The week of exams passed in almost total silence; a week of watching other candidates rubbing up acquaintance; a week of wondering about the very confident looking owner of the rather gloomy room, who appeared on several sporting photographs hung on the walls; a week of dining in the old hall out of shiny metal dishes on highly-polished, clothless tables. My failure to win even a place was at once a disappointment and a relief.

However, St. Catherine's College held its scholarship examinations two months later, in the schools themselves. As we had been taught from the entrance papers for almost a year, this time I was able to pull off all the old tricks. I won an Exhibition and during that last few months of the sixth-form, basked in the glow of being one of nature's elect. We very few open award winners were in one way the school's only real successes.

Cambridge was all my parents could have wished. They came to see me during the second Long Vacation and found supreme happiness sitting on the Backs looking over the river and towards King's College. For my father, Lord Mauleverer (of Billy Bunter and *The Magnet*) might have walked that lawn; Tom Brown must have been there, and the Fifth Form from St. Dominic's. He had read *The Adventures of Mr. Verdant Green at Oxford*, and saw that I had a 'gyp' (as Verdant Green had a 'scout'). He imagined how my gyp would shake his head and say (as Verdant Green's scout *always* said), 'College gents will do anything.' All I could say—and I said many bitter things— couldn't convince my parents that that powerful Cambridge image of my father's schoolboy reading wasn't *my* Cambridge. 'We'll have to start learning to talk proper now,' my father would quip, not wholly joking. How I writhed when he asked me, not completely facetiously, how soon Lord Mauleverer was coming home with me! How I ranted when my parents and family listened to Union debates on the wireless, watched 'our boat' in the Boat Race, or waited eagerly for 'our team' to score in the Varsity Match! To no effect. Actually, the only Public-School friends of mine they met seemed to them comically distasteful. But they never lost their dream. I came slowly to accept that when I questioned it, just as when I expressed my doubts about a scientific future, they became frightened,

118

hurt or puzzled, and said that I had a funny attitude to things.

I was probably the more bitter in self-reproach because for a while I had enjoyed the status in the family which my Cambridge place had brought me. Everyone was very proud of me, although there was a slight edginess about close relationships. It was a compliment to say that Cambridge hadn't changed me. They would look at me guardedly, testing me out: 'I expect you'll be a Con. (Conservative) now, then,' not altogether accepting my assurances to the contrary. In a fumbling, uncomprehending way I tried to enter the Cambridge world for them. For after waiting so long and working so hard, if this was to be the reward I felt I must make shift and grasp it. So I forced myself to take some excruciatingly embarrassing dancing lessons. I carefully positioned myself near the prettiest girl in the class during physics practicals. I used to write home about how many times I had given or received coffee. I seriously considered joining the Union. I had some vague notion that it was as important in Cambridge life as the debaters themselves thought. I rowed, and went to a boat-club dinner, learning uncomfortably how to drink. I made a point of taking tea at the cruising club once a week. I felt I ought to go to a May Ball, and wondered how I could help with the Rag. I bought *The Night Climbers of Cambridge*, and it gave me a curious thrill, probably far greater than a Public Schoolboy would have felt, for the consequences of expulsion for me were unthinkable. I bought a blazer and cavalry-twill trousers. In short, I skirted the walls of my father's Cambridge, such of it as I could see, and tentatively essayed whether I would be welcomed in.

I found quickly that entry was not so easy. Unfortunately I found less quickly that entry to that Cambridge wasn't necessary or even important. That Cambridge, Lord Mauleverer's, was there all right, but it remained supremely indifferent to my existence. I never plucked up courage to go to a dance or speak to the pretty girl in physics (she was, I subsequently discovered the daughter of a chairman of the B.M.A.). I discovered later that several friends of that time were homosexual, although then I had no conception of what that meant in terms of living

119

relationships. I didn't make many friends. Yet how quickly all those very large Public Schoolboys called Charles or Miles or Giles or Jeremy, struck up acquaintance and hailed one another loudly across street and quad! In a twinkling they were internationals or Blues (indeed it emerged that they had virtually been *invited* to Cambridge for their sporting skills rather than having to battle their way in through the Opens). I never rowed above the sixth eight: I soon discovered I had neither the physique nor the time. I played rugger, but only with the rabbits. My blazer felt too long, my cavalry twill trousers too short. I was snubbed in the cruising club—and heavily patronized by the club steward there who soon saw I wasn't like the other gentlemen. I had to wait three years for admission to the swimming club; and then there was the awkward moment when it became obvious that my admission had been held up for reasons other than my swimming ability. In my digs, my landlady fed me with questioning accounts of her previous young gentlemen, with their Indian Army parents, and partners with glorious May Ball dresses. Even more difficult to cope with were her approving stories of how the other lodgers had no 'side' and liked to come out into the kitchen to play cards with her. These, her eyes seemed to say, were *real* Cambridge men: what kind of creature are you? From being at school one of nature's chosen few I had become overnight at Cambridge a C-streamer.

I felt all the more a C-streamer because of my work. Now I realized I was not destined to be a Cavendish or Rutherford or Kapitza. Stuck in the ruck of bottom seconds, I would become an oil-engineer, routine atomic-scientist or soap- and fertilizer-maker. When I attempted to change my subject, the College promptly threatened to withdraw my scholarship and hence my grant. There was profound gloom at home. After this, science studies became merely a time-spinning device for stopping at Cambridge. I still hoped and worked, but never again expected to do well. Nevertheless, I played for time by choosing a two-year Part II, which meant that I got a fourth year at Cambridge.

In Huddersfield during the vacations I went to a jazz club where ex-grammar-school pupils congregated, and there I felt lion enough. Jazz, and beer, I took not for themselves but as an emotional release. The casualness, transience, lack of thought for the morrow, all were a revelation. With my new-found Dutch courage, I walked a girl home, and kissed her (but she was not a grammar-school girl and I and my parents secretly found her common). On Sunday evenings the jazz-club group would go singing in the little country pubs where local choirs met for a quiet pint. The sheer enjoyment of this side of life, sadly lacking in my approach to formal education, gave a sort of hope. I began consciously to try to crack the mould into which I was being squeezed. It was, I suppose, a very much delayed adolescence, one which my parents mistrusted exceedingly.

I nearly didn't return for the fourth year. I was due to spend a term at Cambridge doing practical work in the middle of the Long Vacation, but I returned home after only three days to the alternative life which was beginning to build up in Huddersfield. My parents were appalled. They found my attitudes 'hellish', and half concluded (after consulting the *Home Doctor Book*) that I was going mad. However, I did return to Cambridge, at the end of the summer, defiantly sporting a beard, and I finished Part II of my degree.

At first the anti-Cambridge swing went too far. I joined with other ex-working-class boys and we formed a small mutually supporting group, going drinking down the Mill Road, discovering for the first time that Cambridge had a working-class all its own. I got to know *foreign* students in College. But in that final year something seemed to connect. I began to see all around me for the taking that other worthwhile Cambridge which had its allegiances and values elsewhere than in muscular Christianity and gentlemanly conduct. For the first time exhibitions, concerts, plays seemed to be there for me also. Prior to this my interest in music had been partly an escape, partly literally food for the senses so starved in an academic education. Now music seemed not just a frill or an eccentricity, but something central. Also, thus far there had been no communicating door between my reading for pleasure and academic work. I now began to recognize, from people whom I met in College, that there were subjects which one could enjoy doing. And it dawned on me that I could go to lectures and read books in university subjects other than science. This revelation of involvement—which the school had somehow never given me—more than anything else sapped my will to continue with science a day longer than I had to. And the strain of finishing the course left its mark. I had begun to develop bad headaches during examinations, each ordeal seeming worse than the last. I despised my tutors and students who were good at science, dubbing them automatons. Even now once or twice a year I still have the same nightmare. In this dream my free flight away from science has been brought up short, and I am closed again in a classroom or lecture theatre, while yet another science lesson drones suffocatingly by.

By that final year I had learned that the Boat Race need not be my Boat Race. But this was only a beginning, and it came almost too late. Politically I was not yet awake or involved, above the continuation of vague family Labour sympathies.

After Cambridge I avoided going into science by effectively spoiling each interview I attended. For I had to insist that Chemical Engineering was not the most important interest of my life. So the Army took me, and here I had more time to read. Among the standard unit-library books was Beatrice Webb's *My Apprenticeship*; and very slowly, with this as a focus, my reading took shape. I came out of the Army on a wave of interest in the sociology of working-class life which Richard Hoggart's *Uses of Literacy*, the Bethnal Green surveys by the Institute of Community Studies, and *New Left Review* helped to arouse and disseminate. Drawn to Bethnal Green both by this and the associations of Beatrice Webb with Charles Booth's poverty surveys in that area, I went to live at Toynbee Hall, a university settlement in Stepney, while I taught on supply at a very rough secondary-modern school near the Elephant and Castle.

Teaching, taking charge of my destiny almost for the first time at the age of twenty-four, was very hard. In a letter to Michael Young at the Institute of Community Studies I explained my position as well as I could at that time, and I was offered initially a part-time job taking round questionnaires. A year and a half later, after four or five such small jobs I achieved temporary security in sociology for the first time when, with Brian Jackson, I worked on the survey for *Education and the Working Class.*

Looking back now at my social work and teaching from Toynbee Hall, and the sociological investigations which have followed, it is tempting to see a pattern. Almost as the young Oxford undergraduates in the settlements had done in the last century, I was coming to grips with the working-class for the first time. My breakthrough had not been a struggle out of the working-class. It had been an endeavour to see clearly through the respectable glasses that my upbringing and education put on me. The story has gone some way towards a happy ending. It is six years since I had any unemployment stamps on my card. Family relationships have mellowed, and become cordial with the birth of my children. For I married a girl whom I met at the jazz club when I went back to work in Huddersfield. It is tempting to finish my story here.

But this would be misleading without a postscript. My education has left nagging doubts about my personality and potential. For instance, should I have done more for myself than I did? In commencing on the system which has produced me, am I merely giving a personal world-picture—or transferring to the outside world what are basically failures in family relationship? Huddersfield still at once draws and depresses me in a way I find very difficult to define. The self-contemplation of the present essay, and *Education and the Working Class,* provide one sort of answer; time may bring more. But although I am thirty-three years old, to end with a flourish, 'look I have come through', still seems premature.

VIII

JANE MITCHELL

Lecturer in Classics, University of Reading

The house where I was born in 1934 is just behind Hampden Park Football Stadium. We lived at the inner edge of a large estate built by private enterprise in the 1920s on the southern outskirts of Glasgow. There were three types of house, clustered in fairly clearly-defined areas, and referred to locally as 'Toytown, Ticktown and Tintown.' 'Toytown' and 'Ticktown' were in the centre and consisted, respectively, of owner-occupied bungalows and 'semis'. We lived in 'Tintown' and these were rented maisonettes, built in blocks of four, two up and two down, with a small patch of garden. The upstairs flats of adjacent blocks shared an outside staircase, wooden and slippery in wet weather, with a concrete slab at the foot. When I was about three, I fell from top to bottom of this stair, surprisingly without serious injury. We moved, on Coronation Day, 1937, to a similar house, two streets away, and off the main road; my parents had been afraid that I might run out into the stream of traffic. I remember waving a Union Jack and watching my father load our furniture on to the open lorry which he drove for L.M.S. Railways.

The new flat was held to be superior in that it had an interior staircase, leading directly up from our own front door. I fell down *this* staircase in the middle of my Higher Leaving Certificate examinations. My spectacles were rushed to an optician for urgent repair, ointment was daubed on the cuts and bruises on my face, and when I reached the school for my next examination two days later, the headmaster and the Classics master were waiting anxiously for me on the front steps; I was the first pupil from the school to take the 'Highers' in Greek. At the time of my birth, there were already six people living in our four-roomed flat, my parents, two aunts and an uncle, and my half-brother. My mother was the second of a family of six, of whom one died young. When she was about fifteen, and recovering from rheumatic fever, her mother died, and my mother took over the running of the household. In her late twenties, after her father's death, she married my father, a widower with a seven-year-old son. The family continued to live with her. Gradually, they married and moved out, one brother, an epileptic, a year or so before I was born; another brother and a sister by the time I was four. The remaining sister never married. She had been engaged, during the First World War; her fiancé lingered on with gas-wrecked lungs in a sanatorium for a year or two after the war, then died. She lived with my mother for the rest of her life. I shared a bedroom with her. It was about eleven feet by six, and opened directly off the main living-room.

My half-brother was already thirteen when I was born. I was virtually an only child; and as I had been born with a slight malformation of the breastbone and had bronchial trouble when I was only a few months old, I was considered delicate. I came in for a good deal of indirect spoiling, but was never allowed to be the focus of interest in any family gathering. This suited me well enough, for once I had begun to read I preferred to occupy myself with my own amusements.

I can remember not being able to read. A particular moment is fixed in my memory. It must have been winter, because the electric light was on; it was after we had moved house, and I must have been getting on for four years old. I was kneeling in front of a chair, with one of my brother's old story-books on the cushion. The jacket had a bright orange background and a picture of boys running; but when I opened the book, I found only white pages with rows of incomprehensible, very black marks. I recall very clearly my feeling of rage and frustration. I insisted on being taught to read. I have dim memories of early lessons in spelling out the captions in the coloured comic strips in our Sunday paper. Soon I had progressed to a storybook of my own, in which the stories of 'Puss-in-Boots' and 'Aladdin' made most impression. Reading became my main interest, but I would also spend hours with a wooden tray and a box of dominoes, building imaginary towns, using Ludo counters as people, and making up my own stories.

By the time I went to school, I was already reading fluently. I used to read ahead through the pages of the primer, while my classmates were struggling through simple sentences. As a result, I frequently lost the place, and was rebuked when called upon to read, but rebuked only mildly. In retrospect, I think my early teachers showed a good deal of indulgence. For many years, my mother kept a note written by my class teacher when I was six. The exigencies of war-time had led to our being taught in half-day shifts, girls in the morning, boys in the afternoon. I had been told to come back one afternoon to remedy some faults in handwriting. My mother made me practice for most of the lunch-hour. As it had been arranged for me to go with my aunt to buy a present for my mother's birthday, permission was asked for me to leave half an hour before afternoon school ended. The teacher's reply—often quoted by my mother—included the remark, 'Jean has a remarkably keen brain, but her handwriting will always pull her down.'

In fact, I was always something of a rabbit in any activity involving manual skill or physical agility. I was self-conscious about this, and felt rather an outsider among my class-mates. This, however, was merely one more factor in a pattern of isolation that had begun to develop even before I went to school. I did play sometimes with other children; but in general I found books much more interesting. My mother's constant concern for my health kept me indoors whenever the weather was at all inclement. I did not mind. There were some books in the house: a one-volume encyclopaedia that had belonged to my brother; a book of 'Wonders of the World', full of photographs of foreign places, with travelogue commentary; some books of stories for boys; and, until 1940, when they were donated to the Forces, a number of novels. I had been unaware that these last were in the house. They were unearthed one day from an old chest and sent off a few days later. I recall my indignation; I had had time to read only a few, one of which was *Oliver Twist*. One or two were kept back—old school and Sunday school prizes—*The Wide, Wide World, John Halifax, Gentleman, Robinson Crusoe* (unabridged), and these I read several times over. Gradually, I acquired books of my own, starting with a junior encyclopaedia in eight volumes, which was bought not long after I started school. Books were my favourite birthday and Christmas presents.

I started school, in February 1939, in a 'temporary' building which was still in use long after I left the secondary part of the school in 1951. The new building was officially opened on September 4th, 1939—and promptly closed for six months to act as a temporary centre for refugees and evacuees. For the first year after it re-opened, we were taught for half a day only. All this, plus the usual succession of childish ailments—measles, mumps, whooping-cough and chicken pox—and a succession of long-lasting chest colds, gave me plenty of time on my own at home to pursue my main passion. I have very poor eyesight today. The foundations for this were probably laid when I was recovering from measles, and insisted on being allowed to start reading again. As I continued to progress well at school, it was almost two years after this before it was discovered that I was short-sighted; and by that time I was *so* short-sighted that there was a period of alarm in which I was taken off to Corporation eye-clinics for one examination after another, until it was established that there was no serious damage to my eyes, and spectacles were prescribed.

After measles, it was discovered that my heart action had become irregular. More clinic visits, more specialist tests, and no organic damage was found. My parents were assured that I would grow out of it—and I did, eventually—but it meant more isolation. I had to avoid strenuous physical activity. This suited me, for it meant that outside school hours I could stay mainly at home and read. My natural laziness was encouraged; and I began to put on weight. This plumpness persisted throughout my teens. I came in for a good deal of teasing from my contemporaries, based partly on my physical awkwardness and partly on my academic prowess. I soon discovered that children don't like swots.

It was apparent from an early stage in my school career that

127

I was a bright child. My mother made it clear to enquiring relatives that there would be no question of my being taken away from school when I reached leaving age. She was made very angry by any suggestion that education was wasted on a girl, who 'would only go and get married'. I think that privately she considered marriage and a career incompatible; but I was to be given my chance of the latter. My father, always the less vocal of the two, agreed with her. There was no fussing or nagging about my school-work. My parents felt themselves unqualified to intervene, and, in any case, I patently needed no pressing. At secondary school, they left the choice of specialist subject to me. I was good at everything, and they rather enjoyed the chagrin of the teachers whose subjects I dropped, regarding this as a testimony to my ability. They had no notion, at this stage, what careers would be open to me, except that it was clear that I could go on to take a degree and perhaps become a school-teacher. This would have satisfied their ambitions; but they made every effort, including the acceptance of financial strain, to ensure that I should receive as much education as I was capable of. I did in fact stay on at school to take my 'Highers', and then got two first-class degrees—one at Glasgow, one at Oxford.

I doubt if I would have got my Oxford First had I gone there at eighteen years old, instead of twenty-one, for I had little scope in my school-days to develop any critical approach by discussion of what I read.

At home, there was little conversation, and that mostly of an anecdotal kind. My father, born in 1896, one of the nine children of a night-watchman, had left school when he was twelve. He had not been interested in school, and had not done particularly well. To the end of his life, his grammar remained shaky, his reading and arithmetic slow and uncertain. In the reorganization after the nationalization of the railways, he was for a time concerned in a 'rationalization' scheme, which involved preparing reports on the volume of lorry traffic to and from particular stations in Glasgow. The composition of these reports cost him a great deal of effort and worry. They sometimes brought back the nightmare which he had had after being in the trenches during the First World War, and which had recurred during the Clydeside blitz. He always drafted the reports on scrap paper, and had me correct them. He had an enormous respect for people with 'brains' and technical qualifications, and perhaps exaggerated his own shortcomings. He was very shy outside the circle of his family and workmates. When parents' meetings were held at school, it was invariably my mother who attended, alone. When he was offered the presidency of his bowls club, he refused; it would have meant speaking in public. I never saw him read anything other than a popular newspaper, or an occasional light novel when on holiday. He preferred to spend his evenings playing bowls in summer or dozing by the fire in winter; he paid little attention to the radio.

Yet he had qualities which, given better opportunity for development in early life, could have brought him considerable success in positions of greater responsibility. Though hot-tempered, he was without malice, and his work-mates liked and trusted him. He was painstaking and methodical. Starting as a railway carter (by the time I was born, the horse had been replaced by a lorry, but he still wore the traditional, stiff black-leather leggings), he made a point of noting exactly which streets were served by the station to which he was assigned. Over the years, he extended this to all the local stations in Glasgow, taking in the new estates as they were built, and stations in outlying parts of the conurbation as well. The results of this work he compiled in a fat note-book, which eventually became a series of notebooks, written out in block capitals and carefully cross-referenced. At the end of the war, he was made foreman of a goods station on the west side of Glasgow, then of the main goods-station north of the Clyde. Finally, he was promoted to the lowest grade of 'salaried staff' (meaning that he got paid fortnightly instead of weekly); his job was to check the return-sheets of drivers delivering over a large part of the north side of the city and to maintain liaison with the principal business firms concerned. One agreeable perquisite was a large bundle of comics and magazines—of the *Red Letter* and *Family Star* variety—every week from a printing firm. For this job, he was earning at the time of his death in 1957 about £500 a year. His 'index' had become known; once a year, at the time of the great

Glasgow Fair holiday rush, he was seconded for a fortnight to Greenock. There, the luggage of Clyde coast holiday-makers was piled up in a great warehouse. My father's encyclopaedic knowledge was put to use in sorting the stuff for delivery to local stations.

My mother, born in 1900, was considered bright at primary school; but there was no money to spare for secondary education. Instead, she was allowed to stay on after the age of twelve for a two-year supplementary course, which consisted of little more than domestic science, arithmetic and some English. The rheumatic fever followed so closely by her mother's death meant that she went straight from school to housekeeping, and never took a job. She was fonder of reading than my father, but had little time or energy to spare for it outside holidays. She read newspapers with a keen attention for anything—such as new national insurance schemes or Council rates increases—likely to affect the family budget; apart from that, she was content to follow stereotyped attitudes. She and my father both voted Tory. While at Oxford, I joined the Labour Party. Thereafter, she would occasionally in letters deliver her opinions on various political issues, usually in the fairly recognizable terms of her favoured newspaper. I seldom attempted argument, as she refused to budge from her position. At the same time she found in my Socialism a source of pride, since it was for her a symbol of my having entered a society of intellectuals.

I saw too little of my half-brother to get to know him well. He often worked night-shift at the G.P.O. teleprinter office. From 1942 to 1946 he was in the army. A year after his return he was married and no longer living with us. He had been quite bright at primary school, and had won a place at a Senior Secondary school. As his birthday fell in January, he transferred at an earlier age than was usual. He showed some ability in mathematics and science, but insisted on being allowed to leave school at fourteen, and got a job as a G.P.O. messenger-boy. My mother was disappointed, but made him attend evening classes. He took courses in, I think, mathematics and electrical engineering. He became a teleprinter operator, still with the G.P.O., and did very much the same sort of work during his military service with the Royal Corps of Signals.

After the war, he returned to Glasgow G.P.O., spent some time with teleprinters, and then was instructor in the school for telephone operators. In 1955, he moved to a large English city as assistant telephone sales-manager, then a few years later to a nearby town as head of its telephone sales office. His two sons are now at grammar school, and will be staying on to take 'A' level.

My aunt was the most talkative member of the household, producing a stream of anecdotes about people in the neighbourhood from bus-queue gossip, about the assistants in the shoe-shop where she was charge-hand, and about the various relatives and acquaintances living in the area, near Glasgow Cathedral and now mostly gone through slum clearance, where the shop was situated. Oddly, she was our main source of information on the activities of most of my father's brothers and sisters. My father was the offspring of a 'mixed marriage', which in Glasgow meant Catholic and Protestant. Some of the children had been brought up in one faith, some in the other (my father was in the Protestant section) and they had tended to drift apart in adult life.

These stories distracted my aunt's attention for a time from her personal health. She brooded over minor ailments, but could seldom be persuaded to consult her doctor about them. When she had exhausted the current day's news, she would retire to the bedroom to change the dressings on the ulcerated leg which troubled her for many years.

Our social circle was small. There were rare meetings with relatives. On alternate Thursdays, my mother and a group of four female friends took turns to visit each other for tea and I used to go along after school. An old lady, who had been our neighbour, was visited on alternate Wednesdays. The main attraction of these visits, for me, was the opportunity to find some unfamiliar reading matter. I liked hearing the old lady's reminiscences of her childhood and of her career as a soprano with a touring concert party. She had even been to America. Her husband was a retired master plumber, as gentle and quiet as she was loquacious and imperious. I was impressed by his wavy grey hair and by the fact that he had won shooting prizes at Bisley. I also found a good deal of interest in his copies of

Reader's Digest. But in general the conversation going on around me afforded little food for thought. At school, too, the emphasis was on learning rather than discussion. My primary school had classes of more than forty-five in number and we were drilled in the three 'R's by traditional methods. Discipline was strict. One class teacher whom we had for the last two years before the selection examination, was so ferocious that we dared not move a muscle, even when she unbent so far as to read us a 'Just-So' story. Nevertheless, I enjoyed the mental drill and exercise I was put through, even the memorizing from our geography book of the principal rivers and promontories of the British Isles, going round the coasts clockwise, and the principal towns, with the products appropriate to each. Arithmetic I enjoyed as an agreeable game, and made it a point of honour to do as much of it as possible mentally. For a year or two, I had what was almost a tic—I would go around compulsively factorizing and multiplying numbers in my head—dates, bus-ticket numbers, anything. I still find myself doing this. I worked out for myself the methods of determining without division, whether a given number is divisible by three, or by eleven. The year 1944 fascinated me, because it was $3^5 \times 2^3$. The rules of grammar and spelling I learned obediently, as a matter of rote, though I had never seemed to have any trouble with either. It never occurred to me to question the purposes or methods of what we were made to do at school. The stuff was there to be learned, and I enjoyed mopping it up.

The same conditions very largely persisted through my secondary schooling. After the selection examination, at the age of twelve, I went on to the Senior Secondary (roughly the equivalent of grammar-school) which was in the same building as the primary school. I cannot remember my parents ever expressing any anxiety beforehand about the results of the examination. I felt nervous just beforehand; not about passing—I had no formulated doubts about that. My anxiety was about the possibility of doing fifty mental-arithmetic problems in forty minutes. This was one of the three papers. We had been given some drill, using old papers and I had found that I could not do it *and* produce my best handwriting; and our teacher laid great stress on the virtues of neat work.

There were three papers: one in mental arithmetic, one in arithmetic, showing the working; and an English paper which consisted entirely of questions of the type 'tick one of the following'. I made one silly error in each of the three papers, a falling from grace which annoyed me intensely, and came up with a score of 147 out of 150 marks. I was particularly cross with myself over the error in the English paper. The word given was something like 'varied' or 'multicoloured'. I hesitated between 'homogeneous' and 'heterogeneous'—and ticked the former. Immediately after the examination, I looked up 'Villette', which I had just read, and found 'heterogeneously' in Chapter 8, in a context which left no doubt as to the meaning. I could have kicked myself.

In the course of the first year at secondary school, we were subjected to two intelligence tests. I don't know how I fared in these. At the time, I thought them ridiculously easy, but suspected that I had gone wrong several times through being over-ingenious.

I enjoyed all the new subjects which now appeared on the time-table. The teachers were all busy coping with large classes, but a number of them lent me books to read on my own—especially English, French, Science and translation of classical authors. I devoured these, and made twice-weekly visits to the public library as well, where I tended to borrow only novels, poetry, plays and the occasional work on literary criticism. Most of this reading remained undigested, as there was little chance for discussion. This also meant that there was little occasion for me to attempt to formulate my own ideas and express them. This is something that still, after an Oxford Greats course involving the writing of two essays a week, and after several years of university lecturing, I find very difficult. I find it much easier to follow the development of someone else's exposition, or to niggle on points of detail, than to produce any construct of my own. To use the terms of Bernstein's social linguistics, at home, I heard only 'public' language; at school, I had no difficulty at all, thanks to my reading, with the 'formal' language used in exposition by teachers; but I had little opportunity to *use* formal language.

My decision to be a classicist resulted from a combination of accident and instinct. As a small child, I had read versions of stories from Greek and Roman legend and history and found they had a strong appeal, of a kind which I could not specify, but which was not a romantic appeal. At secondary school, I was in the 'A' stream, and when I had been learning French for a year, I was given the option of starting German or Latin as a second language. I chose Latin, and was at once captivated by its sound and its beautifully logical structure. At the beginning of my third year, a new Classics master came to the school, a tall, beetle-browed man from Stornoway, of whom we stood much in awe. He took me aside one day and asked what my favourite subjects were. I knew that at the end of the third year, after the Junior Certificate examination, we were obliged to specialize. All I can remember of my reply is that I found mathematics too mechanical, and that I wanted to go on with Latin. A day or so later, having consulted the headmaster, my Classics teacher told me that I'd better start learning Greek; and was I very religious? The answer being 'No', he at once began to give me Greek lessons in the twenty minutes that were allowed at the beginning of the school day for marking the registers, saying the Lord's Prayer, and indulging in whatever vaguely religious activity might commend itself to the form-master or mistress. One teacher used to resort to making the class parse the Lord's Prayer; another read to us from books with titles like 'Ten Lives that shook the World'. Occasionally I rushed back to school after dinner, and we fitted in another twenty minutes before afternoon school.

At the end of the third year I had to 'specialize'. English, Maths, French and Geography/History were compulsory. I dropped Science, Geography and Art. There was some repining on the part of those teachers whose subjects I had dropped. Some of the others expressed regret, as it was clear that I would not go on to study their particular subjects after leaving school. It was assumed that I would go on to Glasgow University, as did a handful of pupils from the school each year. I was now carrying one extra subject, although no more, I later discovered, than was normal in the 'fee-paying' private schools in the city. The headmaster therefore saw to it that I had special time-table arrangements for my last two years at school. Periods were docked off other subjects to allow Greek to be fitted in. In French, for instance, I had only two periods a week in the fourth form, and three in the fifth, as against the normal five. Nonetheless, I did all the class-work and managed a good deal of extra reading as well. I was even, on one occasion, found reading a borrowed copy of the *Hotspur* comic under the desk in one of my two French periods, but I was able to demonstrate that I was already considerably ahead of the work scheduled. At home, the sitting-room, with a gas-fire, was put at my disposal for homework. There was little or no traffic noise outside. The radio in the living-room was sometimes audible, but my parents would turn it down when asked. In summer, there was a good deal of noise from children playing in the street and from the tennis-club opposite. However, my mother liked to spend summer evenings at the sitting-room window, watching the tennis, and my father was usually out at the bowling-green, and I was able to use the living-room instead.

In the third form, with a number of my class-mates, I was entered for the Hutcheson Trust Bursary, a competitive examination open to all the schools in Glasgow and district. I came first in this examination, and I knew that I would have to try to do the same later in the University Bursary Examination. I suffered agonies of anxiety before the examination, as I felt that the reputation I had won at school would now have to be maintained against unknown outside competition.

The prize was a grant of £15 a year for the remainder of my attendance at school. My parents had already applied for, and been allowed, a Corporation maintenance grant of £22 a year. This was not tenable together with the Bursary, and so there was a family conference. My mother said firmly that the honour was what counted, so we let the grant go and accepted the Bursary. The first instalment of £7 10 0 was spent on a bookcase, which I still have. My father, on his rounds, searched in all the second-hand shops till he found it, a large and splendid glass-fronted mahogany case.

That same year, I entered the junior section of the Glasgow Dickens Society annual competition. One had to answer a questionnaire and write an essay on one of Dickens's novels. In 1949, the work set was *Barnaby Rudge*, and I got first prize.

Next year, I repeated the success in the senior section, on *Our Mutual Friend*. The examination was held on a Saturday morning in Glasgow High School, which was a private school for boys. I remember my surprise at the poky, dark classrooms and dim, tiled corridors of this exalted establishment. My own L.E.A. school had enormous windows, bright paint and verandah corridors.

These successes were gratifying, but my main reaction was one of anxiety. I felt that an expectation was being created in the minds of my family and teachers that I would go on doing this sort of thing. I was conscious of a rather ambivalent attitude on the part of my class-mates. While feeling a certain pride in me, they were nevertheless jealous, especially when I consistently carried off the class prizes. They did not conceal a certain triumphant gloating whenever I happened to make an error in class. In these circumstances, to have come second would have seemed to me like failure. In addition, I had no real idea of how good I was. Many years after, my Classics master remarked to me that he had always been impressed by the modesty with which I bore my successes. The fact was that I did not see any grounds for conceit. I knew that I was better than any of the school-mates whom I had known since early childhood; but I did not regard this as providing any real index of my ability.

Money was fairly tight at home, even with the little additional help from the bursary. We always had enough to eat, but there was little to spare for luxuries. Cakes were baked at home, not bought. A week-end joint of beef for boiling was made to last three days, and the stock used for soup. This is a thrifty Scottish habit. I had never eaten roast beef until I moved to England. In between we had mince and stew and sometimes fish. In summer, an economical meal could be got out of a mould of potted meat. Chips were served no more than once a week, as my mother disapproved of 'fry-ups'. Jam was made at home, and fruit was bought in bulk cheaply from the market and bottled for the winter. For many years, my father provided us with vegetables from an allotment.

Clothes had to last a long time. Uniform was not compulsory at school, except for games. However, I wore my gym-slip most of the time, sometimes alternating with a tweed skirt, and hand-knitted jumpers. I had the happy knack of being able to knit complicated patterns while I read. My father had his railway uniform, which was issued regularly. The old one was kept for wear around the house and garden. My mother was not a very skilful needlewoman, but there was a neighbour who would patch sheets, and even cover eiderdowns, for a small charge. Shirts were taken to a shop near Crown Street to be re-collared.

During my last year at school, I caused everyone a good deal of anxiety by embarking on a drastic programme of slimming. By this time, thanks to an aversion for exercise and an excessive fondness for bread and potatoes, I was grossly overweight. My mother had gone so far as to have me fitted with corsets. I bore these for a few months, then rebelled and began to diet. I lost so much weight that everyone began to fear for my health. I turned this to account, for I found that the games mistress acquiesced readily when I asked to be excused from games, particularly as I allowed her to gain the impression that I had received some sort of official sanction in order to do extra work. And so I got out of hockey and netball—which I loathed and for which I had little energy—and found a corner in which to read instead. By this time, my slimming had become almost compulsive, and I was deaf to the exhortations of my family and the obvious concern of my teachers. By the time of my Higher Leaving Certificate examination, I had lost five stones. When, however, I found that my weight was starting to rocket downwards alarmingly, I began to eat again. I put a strain on the family budget for a period by drinking two pints of milk a day, until I brought my metabolism back to equilibrium. My mother remained convinced for a long time that it was fainting, caused by malnutrition, that had made me fall downstairs.

Our financial position was a little easier when I went to Glasgow University in 1951, supported by the Ferguson Scholarship. Every year, an open competition was held for pupils at schools in Glasgow and South-West Scotland. There was a field of about two hundred and fifty, and the first hundred were eligible for scholarships from such funds as were available. The examination was usually taken by pupils who spent an extra year at school after Higher Leaving Certificate, and the top places were usually won by pupils from the private schools. I was entered in 1951, just three months after my 'Highers'. For the first part of that summer term, I was working on my own. The headmaster set me problems in geometry and algebra. One of the English masters set essays, which he discussed with me in his free periods. The classics master gave me texts to read, and dictated notes on 'background'. I was placed first in the examination. The scholarship was worth one hundred pounds a year. In addition, I had a substantial grant from Glasgow Corporation. The university fees, which were not very high, were deducted from this at source, and I handed the rest over to my mother.

At the University I read Classics. The course did not make any radically different demands, except in quantity, from those I had experienced at school. Teaching was by lectures, there were few essays, and no seminars. Whether the Honours part of the English course would have made different demands, and whether I would have been adequate to them, I don't know. I read English as well for the first two years. The classes in those years were enormous, about three or four hundred in the first year, and there was no individual tuition. During the four years of my degree course, I was living at home and travelling in each day, a journey of about an hour each way. I had no very close contacts with other students and took very little part in university life. I felt that I had to devote as much time as possible to work. This was largely true. Anxiety made me work anyway, but I had read fewer Latin and Greek texts than most of my contemporaries, and, for rather complicated reasons, I ended up taking more courses than were strictly necessary. I worked very hard, and acquired a collection of medals and prizes and a First-Class Honours degree. When it was suggested during my last year that I should apply for Oxford, I did. Traditionally, a trickle of students from Scottish universities went on to Oxford or Cambridge. With other subjects, it was possible to go on to an advanced degree at Oxbridge; but with Classics, one read another first degree. The first part of the course at Oxford was basically the same as the Glasgow course, but at the time of my application my Oxford college refused to allow me to go straight into Part II. My parents' faces were rather long when it emerged that I would have to spend a further four years at Oxford, but they were proud and pleased that I had been awarded a scholarship.

It was about this time that hints began to be dropped by my mother that she would be glad when I was earning, and could do something to pay her back, and that I should concentrate on my career and not think too soon, if at all, of getting married. At the time, this evoked no particular reaction from me, since I had not envisaged the latter possibility. My ideas on that, as on a number of other topics, changed and developed dramatically after I got to Oxford. During her last years, I felt a real sense of strain in my relations with my mother. So long as I had been the quiet, academic daughter, content to stay at home with her books, she had felt secure. The moment every parent has to face, when a child's independence has to be recognized, had in my case been postponed so long that it was all the more difficult for her when it did come. By the time I left Oxford, she was a widow and I had marriage in prospect. I wrote to her once a week and went up once or twice a year for a visit, but these visits were painful, as the fundamental question of our relationship could never be openly discussed.

I think I first began to mature at Oxford, and this brought a number of personal difficulties, most of which were more or less satisfactorily resolved, helped by the fact that the first five terms' work had a great deal in common with what I had done at Glasgow. I was aware of class differences, but this gave me no feeling of social inferiority. I was unimpressed by affluence, or the fact that some students had been to an exclusive public school. Had I myself come straight from school, I might have been more easily overawed; but with a First-Class Honours degree to my name, I felt I had my own claims to status.

However, I began to feel myself at a considerable disadvantage because of the narrowness of my interests and experience. A chance meeting with a fellow-Scot led to my being introduced to Oxford left-wing circles. Here I was at first completely at sea, and felt abysmally ignorant, but I listened and learned, followed up references to unfamiliar authors and pondered on unfamiliar value-judgments. It was an active time. Suez and Hungary were engaging people's activities and emotions and

139

the New Left was just forming. The magazine 'University and Left Review' began to be produced from a house in Oxford where at all hours groups of people were to be found talking animatedly. It was here that I first discovered that jazz was taken seriously by some intellectuals.

I felt as if an intellectual explosion was taking place in me. This was accompanied by an emotional explosion. I had so far had no experience of dealing with people on other than a formal, superficial level, and had no idea how other people reacted to me. At that time, I must have been pretty insufferable. I used my college for little more than eating, sleeping and working. I discovered later that some of my contemporaries were girls with whom I could have developed valuable friendships, but, at the time, the place grated on me, and I refused to explore its social potential. I felt there was altogether too much emphasis on social life of a frivolous kind, particularly among the girls of the 'debby' set. I didn't envy them; I knew the difference between sweet sherry and dry and didn't give a hang about the social significance of this. I preferred beer and politics.

By the end of the second year I had developed opinions of my own and was surprised to find that I had a reputation for intelligence. I had also, after a series of stormy passages, met a carpenter's son, a first-generation grammar-school boy from Stratford-upon-Avon, with whom I found I had a lot in common. It was soon understood between us that we should marry, as we did four years later after he had completed his doctorate.

I was able therefore to start on the second half of my degree course with more confidence and more emotional balance than would have been the case two years earlier. The work was unfamiliar. Two essays a week had to be written, one in ancient history, one in philosophy. There was no direct instruction on how to tackle the subjects. One learned, by observing the technique of lecturers, tutors and the writers of recommended articles. The only real academic difficulty, if it can be called such, I experienced was a recurrent complaint from my tutors about the tortuousness of my English style. By the last term, some improvement in this respect was discernible.

It could be said that I have had a 'breakthrough' at three

different stages at least of my career. The first was when I started to read, and I was lucky to have been an early developer. At secondary school, I was fortunate to have an enterprising Classics master and a sympathetic headmaster. In so far as my environment created any difficulties for me, it was the lack of opportunity to develop my ideas through discussion. In a sense, I was largely self-educated. This produced a certain narrowness and introversion, and I think it also retarded the development of a capacity for original thought. My Scottish university education did not help much in this respect. The third real breakthrough, starting at Oxford, was when I began to be capable in some degree of articulating my mental experiences. I still do not do this very successfully. It has not prevented me from having, in conventional terms, a highly successful education career, loads of prizes, a First at Glasgow and a double First at Oxford, but the real test comes later, after formal education stops.

I am now married, and a university lecturer. I am becoming progressively more articulate, but I feel I have still a long way to go.

IX

GERALD NABARRO[1]

Conservative Member of Parliament for South Worcestershire

I was born on 29th June, 1913, in Cricklewood, which was then one of the inner suburbs of London and, if the wind was blowing in the right direction, was within the sound of Bow Bells. I might therefore be adjudged a Cockney. I suppose in contemporary parlance it might be described as a lower middle-class area. I was the second of five children and had an elder brother, born twenty-seven months before me, who was killed in action during the Battle of Britain.

The house was red brick, late Victorian, semi-detached, with a small garden in front and behind, lace-curtained windows with an aspidistra in an old art pot. There were three bedrooms, one occupied by my parents, one by my brother and myself and one used as a spare room. It was a modest household, but a happy one, and there was an adequate income for those days. My father was a retail tobacconist and merchant and sold cigarettes under his own name. Of course, I knew little of the social environment, because I was so young.

My earliest memories, at the age of about three, during the First World War, were being taken from my home for walks in the park by my mother and seeing the Red Cross trains running on a loop line of the old Midland Railway. I lived there until 1917 when the Zeppelin bombing made it somewhat uncomfortable. My father moved his family out of London to a house at the corner of Headstone Lane, Pinner, where it leads off to the railway station on the line to Watford. We were there until the end of the war. Later we lived in Hampstead for a couple of years. There my two sisters were born.

[1] Transcribed from a recorded conversation with the editor.

The year 1921 was one of calamity for my father. I was then seven years old, and at that time two things occurred which profoundly affected my life. The first was that my mother died in childbirth; the child, utterly deformed—what we would call today spastic—survived, but my mother died. The second was that my father was made bankrupt in the post-war depression.

For a short while, a few months before the death of my mother, I had been at a preparatory school called Holly Hill in Hampstead, which was the junior school of University College School in Frognal, Hampstead. It was almost a kindergarten and is not really significant in my early education. After my father became bankrupt and with my mother dead, the baby, then a few months old, was taken over by a nursing home and I never saw the child again. Subsequently, he was adopted. We four children were split up among my father's brothers and sisters, and I went to live with my uncle and godfather, Dr. David Nabarro, who was a foremost children's specialist of his day, practising in Harley Street, and head of the Department of Pathology at Great Ormond Street Children's Hospital. He was married to a former nursing sister at Great Ormond Street, Miss Nora Webster of North Walsham, who is alive today and whom I adore. Uncle David was a dominating influence in my life; his cultural influence on me was great and he taught me both moral and material values. He guided me and later during my seven years in the Regular Army he and my Aunt were the only members of my family to keep in touch with me. Dr. David died in 1958 and his long and distinguished career was recorded in 'Who's Who' for many years.

For a while I was brought up by my Aunt and Uncle. Then my father married again, a young woman, and the family, impoverished, with only a few pounds a week—my father was now an undischarged bankrupt—was re-united and went to live first in Ealing and then in Southall, Middlesex. Ealing and Southall were both working-class areas. The house we lived in at Southall is still there, No. 8 Scotts Road. I remember the price of it in those days was £475. It was semi-detached, with a tiny garden at back and front, and a good deal smaller than a modern Council House. My brother and I slept in bunk beds, my brother up aloft and I below, because our room was too small to take two normal beds. During this period, the family was supported by relatives. I was then eight or nine years old.

In Ealing I was sent to Drayton Green Elementary School, West Ealing London W.13, an L.C.C. school, typical of the day, what we would now call a primary school, and then to North Ealing L.C.C. School, a similar establishment. These two schools, still in existence, formed the basis of my early education.

My father's educational background was quite good. He had attended Lady Owen's School, Islington, North London, which is a famous old grammar-school. My paternal grandfather in Victorian times was a diamond merchant in Hatton Garden. He married a lady named Ricardo. My name, Nabarro, is a derivation from the Spanish 'Navarro', my family, some 400 years ago, having transmigrated through Portugal, where the 'v' became transposed to a 'b', then via the Low Countries, to settle in Amsterdam, and later in England. My mother's maiden name was Drucquer and her family were well-to-do business people, living in Manchester. I have little recollection of my mother, only that she was a vivacious, cultured woman, a good musician, tender and kind, fond of children, who reared us well until her untimely death.

Nor do I recall much of my early days at school, except that I didn't do at all well. I was constantly in trouble for laziness and not working and learning. I was not an apt pupil. There were no subjects which caused me special difficulties and generally I liked my teachers, but I regarded school as an oppression. I was unhappy at home due to the changed circumstances and environment, and bored at school. I was anxious to leave, start work, earn money and make my way.

I think my father must have worried and felt I should have gone to a better school, but he was very ill for two or three years, suffering dreadfully from arthritis and unable to work. He was in fact able to follow, only in a desultory sort of way, any occupation at all: he opened a tobacconist's shop for a time after he was discharged from bankruptcy. Later he became a commercial traveller and did rather better. My two sisters were educated at local council schools as well, but they stayed on rather later than I did: broadly, their education was the same as mine. Subsequently one married a manufacturer and the other married an engineering technologist. On my fourteenth birthday, I decided to be done with school. I was then five feet five inches tall and weighed about nine stones. I was a small chap. I had received only the rudiments of education: I could read and write but that was about all. I took a job as an office-boy, for which I was paid twelve shillings and sixpence a week. Then, in the years of depression, I secured a job on an American freighter and went to sea. A kindly Captain took to me and I was put to work in the galley where I earned four shillings a week. I sailed from the Port of London to Newport News, on to Galveston, Texas, then to New Orleans, through the Panama Canal to San Francisco up to Portland, Oregon and Seattle. There I was paid off and I literally starved on the docks and had to beg for something to eat, finding perhaps a half-day or one day's casual work a week. After a few weeks I found work on a coastal steamer sailing to San Francisco where I later picked up a British ship and arrived home after a salutary twelve months at sea. This had a remarkable influence on me. I was still quite small, about five feet six inches tall and rather underweight and still largely ill-versed, but life at sea had broadened me physically and toughened me up.

Then I decided to join the Army. I presented myself to a Recruiting Sergeant at Whitehall and insisted on joining a particular regiment, the King's Royal Rifle Corps (60th Rifles) because I knew that regiment habitually and traditionally recruited small men. They are a regiment of small men, derived from the German Sharp Shooters or Jaegers, historically wearing green and and black tunics. I put my age on by three years, saying I was eighteen. I got away with it; the Army was very short of men and they didn't ask too many questions. I organized references to get enlisted and, after my twelve months at sea, I was very fit and eventually I was attested. The main reason prompting my enlistment in the Army was adventure, but there was more security than at sea. Those were the years of acute depression, it was 1930 and more than two million men in Britain were unemployed. So I went into the Regular Army as a private soldier, or Rifleman. I 'square-bashed' for the first six months, a very arduous training. I remember on my first route march (World War I marching order with a heavy S.M.L.E. rifle) I passed out after a few miles and was supported by a couple of old sweats and carried in. I became a very good shot, particularly with automatic weapons.

Rapidly I grew tougher, stronger and acclimatized: I joined my regiment, the second Battalion of the King's Royal Rifle Corps. I made good progress in the machine-gun company. I was noticed, for the first time in my life, by regimental officers and promoted to Lance-Corporal. In the ensuing years swift progress continued. I was sent on weapons and small-arms courses, a machine-gun course for example, and I started to work really hard. I became a good regimental N.C.O. and, specially important, I was learning the rudiments of commanding men. I became aware that I had been blessed with a good memory and that I could commit to memory long tracts on weapons, notably small arms, so that nobody could fault me in oral or written examinations. My writing was, however, rather crude.

Then came an opportunity for me to advance my formal education. The Regiment sent me to the Army School of Education at Shorncliffe for a Junior Instructor's course, which qualified me to instruct in Regimental History, Map-reading, Topography, Mathematics, and other subjects. I won a distinguished certificate. The course involved a great deal of study, of reading and memorizing and I was helped by the encouragement and friendship of a former Marines' Officer on the staff at Shorncliffe. Later, when I rejoined my regiment, I became an Instructor in the Regimental Schools and on the Weapons Cadre. In view of my earlier very elementary schooling, I had often to turn to better-educated men to help me, but I was lucky in this and progressed well. I sat army examinations for the First-Class Certificate of Education and passed in the five subjects necessary, roughly equivalent to 'O' levels today, Mathematics (involving three papers, Geometry, Algebra and Arithmetic with a certain amount of Trigonometry), English Military History, Imperial and Military Geography and Economics.

Then an interesting event occurred. I had earned quite a good reputation in my regiment and I was made up to acting full Corporal, with two stripes set on my arms at the tender age of seventeen years. Also I disported Machine-Gun Instructor's emblems and marksman's badges. Then followed a senior non-commissioned and warrant officer's long qualifying course at the Small Arms School at Hythe, Kent. Again, I gained a Distinguished Certificate. Only two or three Distinguished Certificates were given on such courses each year, each course having a hundred and fifty sergeants and warrant officers from every regiment of the Army. My results made me a marked man. I was promoted an Acting Sergeant and later a full Sergeant.

From this success sprung confidence and a desire to advance my education. I started reading voraciously, giving up all my spare time to study. Eventually, I decided to enter my name for an external London Matriculation examination. I had realized, for the first time, that education was essential. I assimilated knowledge fast and my Commanding Officer was personally interested in me. He sent me on a long qualifying Senior Instructor's course, six months of military education, again at the Army School of Education, Shorncliffe, where the Commandant, Colonel C. G. Maude, D.S.O., O.B.E., who I believe is still alive today, encouraged and guided me.

From that six-months' course for twenty sergeants from different regiments of the army, I emerged in the top place in the written exams and with a good deal of loosely put together knowledge, which was, I suppose, roughly comparable to sixth-form grammar-school standards. After returning to my regiment, I was immediately posted to Winchester as a Sergeant Instructor. It was in 1934 and I was then twenty years old.

My appetite for learning was really aroused and I embarked on a correspondence course with the Metropolitan College at St. Albans, to try and bring myself up to the standard required for London Matriculation. This involved, when taken externally, six papers, all of which had to be passed simultaneously. At the first and second attempts I failed in one subject—French—and was rather depressed. Fortunately, I was a small-arms marksman and a highly-qualified instructor and the public school, Winchester College, were anxious to win the Ashburnham Shield for their O.T.C., at Bisley, and they knew me in this garrison town. They asked me if I would coach their shooting team in my spare time. I agreed in return for a master at the College cramming enough French into me to reach Matriculation standards. He did, and at the third attempt in one year, I passed. Thus I achieved, at the age of twenty years, an external London Matriculation in six subjects, Mathematics, English, French, History, Geography and Economics. I then sat the Army equivalent of Matriculation, called the Army Special Examination, and eventually passed in nine subjects. All this involved more study and much burning of midnight oil. I did my army duties for six hours a day, and studied for eight hours a day, with little or no leisure. I saved hard. I had raised myself to the contemporary equivalent of four 'A' levels, all in pursuit of my Army career, ultimately with a view to going to Sandhurst and obtaining a Regular Commission. In those far-off days there were about ten commisions a year granted from the ranks, after an eighteen months' course at the R.M.C. at Sandhurst, or the R.M.A. at Woolwich. Candidates seeking entry from the ranks were required to be under twenty-three years of age and to have served in the ranks for two years. They were generally Lance Corporals who had failed the Sandhurst exam at their public schools, from which 95 per cent of the Officers of the Regular Army were obtained. I put in for this 'A' Cadetship from the ranks and since I then had all the educational qualifications and more, the War Office sent me, for my six months' special observation prior to Sandhurst selection, to The Green Howards at Portland. There I served as a Platoon Sergeant and recall with pride the annual march of one hundred and two miles in full marching order, from Portland to Salisbury Plain, for manoeuvres. From there I went for my viva to the War Office and I was accepted for Sandhurst when I was twenty-one. Since the Sandhurst allowance was fifty pounds for uniform and mufti, I had to borrow more money to equip myself properly. Thus, I was due to go to Sandhurst for the eighteen months' course, and then I would have been gazetted Second Lieutenant. At the last moment I was advised against it, because I had no private income. This was, of course, before the Hore-Belisha Army reforms, when ten shillings a day was the pay of a Second Lieutenant. Because mess bills were vastly in excess of ten shillings a day, only gentlemen with private incomes could possibly sustain a Regular Commission, unless they went to the Indian Army where pay and allowances, particularly on the North-West Frontier, were somewhat higher. My intention originally was to serve in the Indian Army and try for a commission in the Gurkhas, Mahrattas, or Punjabis, and soldier in India for life. It seemed to me the sort of life I wanted and I imagined myself a second Robertson, finishing up as a Field-Marshal. I was continuing to work hard in every sense, and had confidence that I could finish high up at Sandhurst. But the economics defeated me and I decided that I would not live in penury for years to achieve this. In great sadness, I decided to leave the Regular Army, which I loved. Anyway, it was my university, and a good one too, rather better than Oxbridge.

I applied to join the Shanghai International Police, a unique body, the minimum qualification for which was to be a full Sergeant in the German, French or British Regular Army. I was a full Sergeant in the British Regular Army and well qualified. The pay was thirty pounds a month in Shanghai 'all found', a princely sum, and the reason men were pensioned for life at the end of twelve years' service was that 80 per cent of them never saw the twelve years through. It was a dangerous job and casualties were high; a buccaneering kind of job and I made up my mind to go out there. But then, the Christmas of 1936 entirely changed my plans.

I had forty-eight hours' leave and I left my station at Larkhill on Salisbury Plain, borrowed a car and drove off to the West of England to find some fun and games on Christmas night and Boxing Day. I stopped off, as it was getting dark, at the Rougemont Hotel at Exeter and changed into a dinner jacket. I went down to the bar and square-pushed the barmaid for a while. Presently, at about 8 o'clock in the evening, an elderly man came in and started talking to me and bought me a drink. We fell to arguing about politics, although I was not very interested in politics then. I was lusty and twenty-two. 'I've my two secretaries here with me,' he said, 'you'd better come and have dinner with us'. I did so and danced clumsily with the two ladies after dinner and went to bed in the early hours of the morning.

The next day, Boxing Day, I got up intending to go out for a walk on the Moors, and I enquired at the desk after the old man. They told me he'd left at 7 o'clock that morning with his two secretaries. I asked who he was and learned that he was the Managing Director of Wilts United Dairies Ltd. and a Director of United Dairies Ltd. I returned to my Regiment and by coincidence, he had been enquiring who I was and had ascertained that I was a regular soldier. Seven days later, a letter arrived from him telling me not to be a fool and throw my life away in Shanghai, and that I ought to go into business. Would I consider letting him give me a job? I wasn't very interested, so I wrote back and refused. Presently, a second letter turned up and I still refused. When the third letter arrived, I replied enquiring what sort of job he could offer me. He said 'Well, you're only fit for a job as a labourer. I'll give you a job as a labourer in my mill in the West of England'. I thought about it and decided to accept. I withdrew my application to go to Shanghai and went to a saw-mills owned by Wilts United Dairies Ltd.

So, my career in business began as a labourer in a saw-mill. My pay was fifty shillings per week, about sixty hours or tenpence per hour. I lodged at Ye Old Poppe Inne at Tatworth, Somerset, where I paid twenty-five shillings per week for bed and breakfast and supper. I walked to and from the mill, daily. After a few months I was noticed by my bosses and put to work on woodcutting machine-tools, and became a machine-hand. Due to the illness of a charge-hand on the night shift, I was somewhat precipitately pushed into running the night shift. They evidently thought I did this quite satisfactorily, because I was shortly appointed a foreman, all in the space of about nine months. Then, I was sent for by the old man who said that one of his saw-mills in London was being badly mismanaged and he proposed to send me there to see if I could do better. I arrived back in London in the spring of 1937, a young man of twenty-three, confident and self-assured, going places, having won my first managerial job, at four pounds a week. I lived in a room in Penywern Road, Earl's Court, and I worked for sixteen to eighteen hours a day, and spent nearly every Sunday at the home of my Uncle and Aunt, Dr. and Mrs. David Nabarro. I used to take my shirts to be laundered by my Aunt and she darned my socks and gave me a good Sunday lunch and tea.

I still loved soldiering and applied for a commission in the Territorial Army. Within weeks I found myself a Second Lieutenant in the Royal Artillery, soldiering with the 51st Brigade, R.A. In my brigade was another Second Lieutenant by the name of Duncan Sandys, who now sits next to me in the House of Commons. Of course, I was on the Regular Army Reserve as a small-arms specialist and machine-gun instructor and as there were then no anti-aircraft guns with which to defend London, World War I machine-guns were pulled out of mobilization stores. But they had no instructors. So presently I found myself posted to a new brigade in Essex, training Territorial Army recruits as a machine-gun instructor. In June, 1938, just before Munich, I was called up and returned to the army as a subaltern to reconnoitre the area of the Thames between Battersea Power Station and Westminister Bridge, with a view to installing large numbers of machine-guns on the tops of buildings, the only defence that area of London would have had against low-flying German aircraft. I performed all these duties, Munich blew over, and then at the end of 1938 I was offered a Regular Commission.

This was a curious coincidence. I had decided earlier not to continue soldiering and now the Army was offering me a commission, without the Sandhurst course. I still thought that there was not going to be a war. I refused the commission and returned to industry. Of course, within months I was re-called to the Army, in August, 1939. Only months later, I was sent out again and placed by the War Office on industrial production duties, and in addition, given charge of the training of thousands of Home Guardsmen in fixed companies for defence of the vital dock area of Liverpool. My industrial responsibilities increased and I found myself running shadow factories, and recorded as 'Unattached List, Royal Artillery, seconded for industrial war production purposes and attached to the Ministry of Aircraft Production'. Later in the war I was responsible for machine-

tool production in Midlands' factories and my industrial knowledge vastly increased. I remained in the Army until 1943, when
I was directed full-time to industrial management duties. I
remained on the Reserve of Officers until 1963, when I finally
severed my connection with the Army, after thirty-three
years.

In post-war years, I have continued as a professional indus-
trialist and businessman, and an amateur politician, which
brings me on to politics and my joining the Conservative Party
in 1945. I was a dedicated, devoted admirer and supporter of
Sir Winston Churchill. Little did I know then that I was to sit
behind him in the House of Commons for nearly fifteen years.
I did not belong to any political party but became interested
due to the nature of my duties in the war, in the tremendous
problems associated with re-settling eight million service men
and women in industry. One evening, shortly before the end
of the war, I was asked by a friend to go along and listen to a
political speech by the Member for Chester, Col. Basil Nield
(now Judge Sir Basil Nield). He had recently returned from the
Middle East and was addressing his constituents for the first
time in four years. I listened to him carefully and half way
through the meeting was passed a note from the Chairman,
who knew me by sight, asking if I would second the vote of
thanks to the Member. He wrote on it . . .'two minutes'. The
lady who moved the vote of thanks got up and thanked the
Member in just twenty seconds, and sat down again. The Chairman put up five fingers to me to indicate 'five minutes' and I
rose and spoke in public, as a civilian, for the first time in my
life. At the end of five minutes I looked at my watch and said
'Ladies and Gentlemen, I have been talking for five minutes
and I conclude by expressing on your behalf a very warm vote
of thanks and welcome home to our Member, Colonel Basil
Nield, M.P.' Some members of the audience shouted out 'Go on,
go on!' So I went on and spoke for another five minutes. Then
I went home.

A fortnight later half a dozen men descended upon me in my
office and asked to see me: I knew none of these men and they
said that at a by-election in Eddisbury, in the early part of
1945, the Government candidate, the Churchill coalition can-

didate, had been defeated by a Common Wealth candidate, that it was traditionally a Conservative seat and would I put my name in for the candidature? I said I had little interest in politics. They said they had heard me speak at this meeting in Chester and wanted me. So I was persuaded to send my name along with forty others. This was for the 1945 General Election, just before the Coalition War Government broke up. When various selection processes had been gone through I was amazed to find myself the Prospective Conservative Candidate for Eddisbury. Within weeks a General Election was declared and it seemed I was on the way to Westminster in a safe Conservative seat which, in the event, was won by a Liberal National, Sir John Barlow.

Just before the Election campaign started, I was telephoned by the Conservative Central Office in London saying that Eddisbury was a Liberal National seat in 1940, and the Rt. Hon. Ernest Brown, M.P., the leader of the Liberal Nationals, had thrown his lot in with Churchill for the General Election of 1945: thus a Liberal National candidate must be selected for Eddisbury and would I withdraw and support Sir John Barlow who was then their nominee? I had no alternative but to withdraw. I turned my back on politics and went back to work.

The following week, I was lunching at the Savoy Grill in London with an old friend, Mr. Edmund Campbell, who said 'Do you know the people sitting at a nearby table?' I replied that I did not. He said one of them was the Deputy Chairman of the Conservative Party, Col. Sir Harold Mitchell, M.P., and would I come and meet him. I was taken over and he said 'You're Nabarro. So sorry about your being squeezed out of Eddisbury'. He went on to tell me that due to the fact that the Conservative candidate in West Bromwich, Staffordshire, had withdrawn and the Election had started, they were without a candidate and would I go up there the next day and be interviewed? So I went off to West Bromwich and sat in a dingy room with forty-seven other people, all chasing the last available Conservative candidature in the country. Once again I was selected. Three days later, in June, 1945, I made my first political speech in the West Bromwich Town Hall. I was defeated on 4th July, 1945, by nearly sixteen thousand votes.

But politics for me had started and, within a few weeks, the Conservative Central Office came to me and asked if I would be the Chairman-elect of the newly founded Young Conservatives in the West Midlands, to try to reverse the younger generation's vote, which had so helped the Labour Party to office. I agreed, and later, confirmed by election, I became the Chairman of the Young Conservatives for the fifty-eight constituencies in six counties of the West Midlands. I was then thirty-two. I worked in industry all day and spoke at political meetings almost every evening. At the end of 1945, quite fortuitous circumstances helped me along once again.

Th distinguished Conservative Member for Solihull, Col. Sir Martin Lindsay, C.B.E., D.S.O., asked me to go and address a tough meeting at a public house in his constituency. I did so and it was an uproarious meeting, very noisy opposition, two-thirds Communist and Socialist in the audience and a very good time was had by all. At the end of the meeting a man came over to me and congratulated me on my performance and said would I please meet his cousin who was Sir Hugh Chance, Chairman of the Kidderminster Division Conservative Association, Kidderminster having been lost to Labour for the first time in history, in 1945. They wanted a candidate to nurse the constituency for four years, and win it back. I went to Kidderminster and briefly expressed my political views. There were about forty-five people, including many defeated Conservative M.P.s seeking the nomination. I think I was probably the only non-Public-School boy. Sir Hugh Chance, himself an old Etonian, told his Selection Committee that he strongly recommended me, a Council school boy who had 'pulled himself up by his own bootstraps'. I was adopted as Prospective Conservative Candidate for Kidderminster and I nursed this constituency for four years, 1946 to 1950.

I used to make about twelve political speeches in a week in those days, half to Young Conservatives in my capacity as area chairman and the other half in the Kidderminster Division, which I hoped to win. At the General Election of 1950 I was elected Member for Kidderminster, winning it back from Labour by 3,805 votes. In 1951 I held the seat by 5,158 votes, in 1955 by 8,224 votes and in 1959 by 9,343 votes. In the New

Year's Honours List, 1963, I was knighted for public and political services, eighteen years after entering politics.

At the end of that year, December, 1963, I had a bad breakdown through over-work and became gravely ill. I was sentenced to complete rest in bed for six weeks followed by many months of quiet convalscence. The election came along in October, 1964, and my constituents in Kidderminster insisted that if I would just write an Election Address, they would fight the election for me by proxy and were confident of getting me re-elected. I said that I had little prospect of being fully restored to health and that it was not fair to them to have a sick man representing them in the House of Commons. I declined, and, in anguish, resigned my seat. I thought my career had ended.

I had sat in four Parliaments as M.P., for Kidderminster for fourteen years and eight months. I spoke frequently in the House and subjected myself to all the rigours of Parliamentary debate. It took me five years to 'arrive' as a Parliamentarian. After that it was easy. I put hundreds of provocative Parliamentary Questions and I addressed meetings all over the country. Because I loved my independence as a back-bencher I refused to contemplate Ministerial office. I televised, broadcast and wrote for the press. It was a life both exacting and exciting but rewarding and I think, useful. All the time my business interests were growing as did my income and the expense of rearing my family.

On Election night, October, 1964, and the following day as the results were coming in, I was invited by the B.B.C. to participate in their commentary along with Mr. Frank Cousins, Mr. George Woodcock, Lord Boothby and several others, which I did. It was the first General Election since the war that I had not been a candidate and I was desolate. Still convalescing and depressed, I bought a passage on a Union Castle ship sailing to South Africa. I spent several weeks in the sun there and in Basutoland. While I was in Cape Town, two extraordinary events happened, the one related to the other.

The oldest university in Scotland is St. Andrews. I had been persuaded, after giving up my Parliamentary seat, to run for Rector. At first I declined for I am neither Scot nor scholar. But fifty per cent of the students at St. Andrews are English and as most of these seemed to want me, I was persuaded. It would have been a very heavy task, due to the work of creating separate universities at St. Andrews and Dundee: three years' hard administrative work, Chairman of the University Court, at which Dons, professors, teaching-staff and students were represented. St. Andrews is six hundred miles from my home at Broadway. There were five candidates including myself and the famous Michael Bentine, but at the last minute Sir John Rothenstein, Director of the Tate Gallery, was nominated and he was, of course, an eminently suitable man to be Rector of a Scottish University. He won by 666 votes to 573. Though my pride was a little hurt at being defeated, I considered it an absolutely merciful deliverance as had I won, I would not be back in Parliament today.

The second event was a cable to me on the ship from my secretary in London telling me that Commander Sir Peter Agnew, the Member for South Worcestershire, had announced that he would not offer himself for re-election at the next General Election whenever it came. My home at Broadway is in the South Worcestershire constituency; it is one of the safest Tory seats in England and contiguous to Kidderminster. With a majority for the Socialists of only three in the House of Commons, it was evident that another General Election would not be long delayed. South Worcestershire was urgently seeking to select a Conservative candidate to succeed Sir Peter. It was being assumed that as I had gone away on a long convalescent trip, I would probably be almost fit again on my return; in my absence, as the 'local boy', my name was being bandied about as a possible successor. But, I was still under doctor's orders, and I cabled back 'No action South Worcestershire'. I was not returning to politics.

Shortly before Christmas, 1964, I returned home and was thoroughly examined by three doctors. Their verdict was my happiest Christmas present: as long as I was careful for a couple of years and did not rush about too much, I would make a complete recovery. We spent a joyous Christmas at home, my wife, our four children and myself. On Christmas night my local doctor came to visit us and said 'You pick up the telephone and tell the Chairman of the Divisional Conservative

Association you are signed off.' I asked 'Why?' He replied, 'Don't ask me why, just do it.'

In the event, the doctor was a strong Conservative himself and on that evening I said that I would not do it. However, on 27th December, 1964, I was feeling depressed: I had been out of the House of Commons for only three months. I telephoned the Conservative Chairman who told me that eighty-six people had put their names in for the candidature, including seventeen ex-M.P.s. They had made a short list of twelve, but now that I might be available, he would ask the Selection Committee to add my name. On that day the third event occurred, because Mr. Geoffrey Johnson-Smith (ex-M.P. for Holborn), one of the twelve, was selected as Conservative Candidate at the by-election at East Grinstead, caused by the elevation to a peerage of Mrs. Evelyn Emmet, M.P. The Chairman phoned back to me forty-eight hours later and said that the Committee had unanimously agreed to accept my name as twelfth man.

Once again I went before a Selection Committee: they recommended me to the short-list of four, three of us ex-M.P.s and one other. I appeared before the Executive Committee of local people, made the speech of my life, a secret ballot was taken and overwhelmingly, I am told, they gave me the nomination, as Prospective Conservative Candidate for South Worcestershire. Thus, for the fourth time in twenty years I had been selected as a Parliamentary Conservative Candidate: at Eddisbury, at West Bromwich, at Kidderminster and at South Worcestershire.

Then followed an extraordinary juxtaposition of events. On a Friday night in January, 1965, my former constituents crowded into the Kidderminster Town Hall to present to me an oil painting of myself executed beautifully by Mr. Edward Halliday, as an earnest of gratitude for my services to them for nearly fifteen years as their M.P. I was deeply touched and the painting has a place of honour in my drawing-room at Broadway.

On the following Monday evening, before 1,400 people, I was formerly adopted as Prospective Conservative Candidate for South Worcestershire in the Winter Gardens at Malvern.

Thus I was translated swiftly from Kidderminster, Worcestershire, to the adjoining constituency of Worcestershire South, my own home constituency. I nursed my new Division for twelve months and addressed, I suppose, a couple of hundred meetings all round the constituency, playing myself in. On 31st March, 1966, Worcestershire South sent me back to the House of Commons, with a majority of more than 11,000, and I have now been back in the Commons for seven months, sitting on the Opposition benches.

I have mentioned my family: happily married in the Cathedral Church of Winchester at the end of the war, Joan, the eldest daughter of Colonel Basil Bernhardt von Brumsey im Thuri, D.S.O., M.C., who comes from an old Austro-Swiss family, originating at Schaffhausen on Lake Constance. The family came to England in the 18th century. My wife was educated at St. Swithin's School, Winchester, and at a finishing school in Paris. She founded, raised and trained the first Hampshire company of A.T.S. under her father who was commanding a Battalion of his county regiment, the Royal Hampshires. The Colonel won the D.S.O. and M.C. early in the First World War, fought right through it, was wounded and mentioned in despatches seven times: a legendary figure in soldiering, a very tough old bird who would rarely accept authority and never got beyond the rank of Colonel. He soldiered for forty years. My wife is personable and cultured and has given me a harmonious and very happy home life.

We have two boys and two girls. The eldest boy achieved a good honours degree in Philosophy, Politics and Economics at Oriel College, Oxford. My second son has started a career in business, working up from the bottom. My two daughters are still at school.

I live in an historic house at Broadway, Worcestershire, a stone Cotswold farmhouse with a lovely garden. My children keep a houseful of pets, ponies, dogs, budgerigars, parrots, hamsters, a tailless cat. His tail was run over by a lorry and Mr. Harold Wilson once referred to our cat 'Jimmy' as a 'synthetic Manx'.

This is all in very sharp contrast to my own childhood and I feel happy, like every self-made man, to have been able to give my children more than I had myself. At the beginning of my career, I resolved that I would be dedicated to creating for my children better opportunities than I had myself. Since I have earned a great deal of money in my life I have bought them the best education that I think money can buy. I may be wrong, but I am pretty pleased with the way they have all turned out. The most important thing, and I am really pleased about it, is that they all have good manners; they are a happy and personable bunch with pleasant personalities and all four are good at games.

As to the future, I believe that men are either born with ambition or without it. My brother, killed in the war, was a douce, studious and unambitious character. I believe that I have largely been his opposite. I have been driven remorselessly by ambition all my life, to excel at everything I do, to work harder than the man next door to me, and to climb in my chosen profession. At fifty-three years of age, it has not deserted me, and much more remains to be done. I do not lust for power: indeed I am rather embarrassed by it and the loneliness it brings. I still prefer the 'spit and sawdust' bar of a public house to the cocktail lounge at the Dorchester. But the driving ambition is there all the time and it accounts for much that I have done, for good or bad, in my life.

Books have become my passion and delight, reading them, collecting and binding them, creating a fine library at my Broadway home. Linked with this I perceived at an early age that I would not really scale the heights unless I could speak fluently. It is the fact that as a Lance/Corporal, I determined to pass out top of all my Army Courses and stood in front of a mirror in an empty barrack room memorizing my Small-Arms Manuals until I knew them faultlessly by heart. I perceived too that I ought to be able to calculate in my head faster than my contemporaries and so I taught myself to do it, quietly and alone, using all sorts of unorthodox methods which I still use to this day.

So when I left the Regular Army, I could talk endlessly and fluently, in pretty good English, though I often used words I had only read and made mistakes in pronunciation. Thus a few years later, political speaking was easy and I memorized speeches before I went onto the platform. On the night before I made my maiden speech in the House of Commons in March, 1950, I was walking around the streets of London for two or three hours memorizing it and then I delivered it without a note. I had always intended to, anyway. I rarely use notes in the House of Commons today, save only scribbled headings on the back of an envelope, and quotations.

Likewise I perceived that many successful men reached positions of eminence without polishing their manners, their behaviour or their way of dress. I bought my clothes in Savile Row twenty years before I could really afford to do so, preferring one swanky suit to two or three less good ones. I had my shirts and shoes made for me because they gave me an air of confidence. I learned table manners painstakingly and how to use a knife and fork, how to choose wines and cigars, and how to conduct myself with propriety at every kind of function from the local Cricket-Club Dinner to the official Banquet. I had to learn to tie a black or white tie before a mirror for hours on end, so that none could ever tell that I had not been taught by my parents how to tie one. Acquisition of some social graces in pursuit of a career is indeed a legitimate recourse. Time and again I have been asked whether I miss the background of Eton and Christ Church. I reply that my education in the 'market place' has served me well and is rather more satisfying. Often acquaintances ask me whether I was at Eton or Harrow, which causes me to indulge inverted snobbery, by responding 'an Elementary L.C.C. School to 14 years'.

X

JOHN PARTON[1]

Professor of Electrical Engineering at the University of Nottingham

---

I was born in Summer Street, Kingswinford, South Stafford-shire. Kingswinford was a fairly old and small village, mostly agricultural, on the southern edge of the Black Country. My father had been employed in the pipe-moulding trade, casting iron pipes, and this particular occupation closed down because the Post Office, who had been using these pipes for their cables, changed over to earthenware ducts. It was a skilled occupation and I suppose my father at that time had a fairly decent wage. My parents certainly owned their house and eventually sold it, for £40 I believe. It was a small cottage with two downstairs rooms, an externally-built kitchen or washhouse, two bedrooms and an attic. It was detached with a large kitchen-garden and some flowers; it was alongside a similar one occupied by my grandmother and an aunt and an uncle, both unmarried. The cottage my mother owned had been left to her by one of her uncles when he died.

When I was nearly two years old, in 1914, we moved to Huntington, a small village in the newly developing coalfield of Cannock Chase. My earliest recollections are of there. There were three or four terraces of about twenty houses each, newly built and in blocks of two and four; we occupied the second house of a block of four. In all there were perhaps a hundred families, mostly miners, but there were a few farms and cottages for the labourers. At that time my father was nearing forty and I suppose one of the reasons he took up mining so late in life would be that it might keep him out of the war; which it did.

[1] Transcribed from a recorded conversation with the editor.

He was never more than a stallman, that is in charge of one or two others, hacking away the coal at the face and loading it into tubs. His daily concern was filling a certain number of tubs in order to make a living wage.

The house in Huntgington belonged to the colliery and we paid a rent of some ten shillings a week. It was about ten yards from the main road and had no garden at the front or at the back; the front door opened straight onto the path. Behind the house, about twenty yards from the back door, there was a siding, twenty or thirty feet deep, for assembling the coal trucks. The house had an outside lavatory with no water; the large cans were emptied weekly by a farmer who used a horse-drawn cart with a large tank. There was a kitchen and two rooms on the ground floor and three bedrooms above; there was a pantry of sorts in the middle of the house and quite unventilated.

We played in the area behind the house; it was of ashes, tipped in from the colliery furnaces. We played football, tip cat, hopscotch, marbles; we fought each other and wrestled; in the dark evenings we swung fire cans. The immediate area about the pit was depressing though it seemed quite natural to me at the time. The country around was beautiful; you could walk out at week-ends on Cannock Chase. There was a lovely pool, Pottal Pool, where we swam most summer days.

I have never checked up on any of the stories about my antecedents. My father's father was a farm bailiff in Stewpony, a few miles south of Kingswinford. He was a lay-preacher, and a very religious man. I do remember him vaguely because he had a malformed thumb. He used to live with our family before we moved to Huntington and then he decided to go to live with one of his other sons in the Birmingham area; he died shortly afterwards. He came from Albrighton in Staffordshire, on the borders of Shropshire, and I believe there are still some Partons in that area. My father was the youngest of five children, four boys and a girl. I knew some of these uncles; one was killed in the First World War; they are all, of course, now dead. The daughter went to work in London, as a model I was told. I never met her but curiously enough four or five years ago, when she died, I received about £66, the only inheritance I have ever had.

My father came from agricultural stock; my grandfather was a bailiff; he had a gun and worked on estates and farms. My father told a story that my grandfather once gave up a well-paid job of protecting a coal yard rather than run-in one of his friends. My father's mother, who was dead before I was born, was a domestic servant and came from Pembroke in Wales.

My mother was one of a family of ten. She was the second of three daughters and there were seven sons. My grandfather, John Cadman, had been killed in a coal mine when she was seven years old. My grandmother, whom I knew very well, had struggled to bring up the children with what help she could get from relatives. The elder children were sent out to work. My mother was a kitchen-maid when she was eleven. When she got married she had been a cook for many years. My parents were married late in life; the first children they had were twin girls, and then another daughter. My mother was forty years old when I was born. There was another girl after me but she died in infancy.

My parents went to elementary schools and paid one penny a week. They both left at eleven years of age. My father said his teacher advised him to stay on but he wanted to get to work. My mother was immensely impressed with education as something she had been denied and firmly believed it to be the means of escape. My father had no strong feelings about education, he did not feel resentful; he neither encouraged nor discouraged. He had an inner belief in personal responsibility and made us all aware that our lives were our own business.

We had no educational help from our parents that I can remember. Apart from the Bible, there were few books. We mostly played cards, draughts and dominoes in the winter evenings. We had a daily paper, and a twopenny weekly *Red Letter*, which had graphic murder stories and love stories; also the *Christian Herald*. The radio came too late to affect our early family life very much. I used to spend most of my summer holidays back in Kingswinford at my aunt's. There, I was very friendly with a boy named Dave Collins. We built several crystal sets consisting of coil, tuning condenser, cat's whisker and head-phones and some were sold for a few shillings. But it wasn't until 1928 or 1929, when all my sisters were away working, that we got a loud-speaker set, with batteries.

For various reasons, one of my sisters was sent to live permanently with my unmarried aunt in Kingswinford and I only saw her at the holidays. The rest of us went to the local school at Huntington until we were fourteen years old. It is difficult to discuss the elder of my twin sisters; she died in tragic circumstances after being for many years a nurse in a mental hospital and in a children's hospital. My other twin sister went into domestic service, married a postal worker and lives in Wolverhampton. She has a family of a girl and two boys. The girl, my niece, is married, has a family, and is a school teacher. The elder of the two boys is at Bristol University taking a degree in Psychology and the younger boy is an apprentice in an engineering concern.

None of us ever went to grammar-school, although the sister who was away almost did, failing to gain a scholarship place only at the interview. She went into a dressmaking firm in Dudley and by the evening-school route and City and Guilds examinations is now in charge of the Domestic Science section of a College in Stourbridge. She has a family of three children, one a qualified engineer, a daughter who is a school teacher and the youngest boy who is in the Fire Service.

I remember little before starting school except fighting a boy who lived a few doors from us. We afterwards became inseparable friends. Another memory is being woken up at night to see the shadowy outline of a Zeppelin. There were many soldiers about in war-time and in post-war camps, and often soldiers were lodging with us.

On my first day at school I am told I distinguished myself by throwing stones in the girls' playground; the area around the school was subdivided by a wall into two playgrounds, one for boys and one for girls. The school consisted of one large building; in it there was one large classroom, subdivided by a curtain, and two smaller classrooms. There were also two cloak-rooms with pegs and a washbasin in each. The toilets were at the bottom of the playgrounds; again no water. Perhaps my earliest school recollection was being in the lowest class, with boys and girls, some older who had stayed down, and a teacher whose name was Miss Webster. She put up a placard with letters on and asked individuals which letters these were; I was moved straightaway into the second class and thereafter I always seemed to be ahead of boys and girls of my own age.

The earliest thing I remember about formal learning was doing square roots when I was six or seven. I always wanted to be learning what my older sisters were learning and this was in the evenings. I don't remember formally being taught to read, and I don't remember being unable to read.

Ours was a Church of England school and had about eighty to one hundred children of all ages from five to fourteen. There were initially four teachers, Miss Webster, two sisters named Miss Bowdler, and a Governess, Miss Greatorex. Miss Greatorex, the 'Guv', was a real terror and wielded authority with a cane and would use it whenever there was an excuse or reason. I was not immune and had a fair share; on the other hand, she obtained a tremendous respect from all the boys. This was a mining village and there were boys in the school who would pick up an inkwell and fling it at the teacher when they felt provoked. She had a hard job to contain these boys, particularly so in that if she took any action against the children that the parents didn't approve of, she could very well be visited by threatening parents. All these teachers lived in Cannock about three miles from Huntington and had to cycle to and fro.

I believe Miss Greatorex was a qualified teacher but the others were not. When I was about eleven and already in the top class, Miss Greatorex left and we had a Headmaster for the first time. The reason was probably that there was some move to introduce fully-qualified teachers. Mr. Rowley, the Headmaster also brought along a Mr. Finlow, who never taught me. By this time two further classrooms had been built. The headmaster made quite an impression on the school and on the village, for we began to be aware of ourselves as a social community. We had scouts (I was eventually a King's scout), we had Whist Drives and Dances; the school had a football team. I remember the joy of being picked to play in the first football team the school ever had and wearing a green-and-red striped jersey.

Educationally the headmaster made little impact on me; I seemed to spend a lot of time in the school garden where incidentally we could grow vegetables to take home. There were examinations to obtain scholarships to go on to grammar-schools which were at Rugeley, Walsall and Stafford. Occasionally a farmer's son would leave our school and be sent at his father's expense to one of these schools; this never made me resentful. In my time no child from our school ever obtained a scholarship to a grammar-school. I went in for a Minor Scholarship twice, once when I was twelve and once when I was thirteen. Neither time did I get considered for a scholarship and most of the time during the examinations I spent wondering what all the questions were about. There seemed to be nothing that I had been taught or could understand. I wanted greatly to go to grammar-school and failed probably because of lack of preparation; teachers would find it difficult to be bothered with an odd student wanting special coaching for an examination. The Headmaster told me after one of these examinations that I had in fact come out at the top of a new-fangled intelligence test.

Arithmetic and mathematics were what interested me most. I remember the beginnings of my scientific interests when Mr. Rowley started us off examining the garden soil to see if it had enough sand, clay and humus content. We used elementary balances and a Bunsen burner. I cannot recall ever doing badly at anything. Just before Miss Greatorex left us she awarded a few prizes, sixpences or so. Although I had won one of these she said she would award it to somebody older as I had plenty of time later to win others.

Poverty was with us all the while. It would strike me most when one of my aunts sent me cast-off clothes from her children. I seemed always to have one good suit for Sundays, and cast-off clothes for the week-days. But we always had enough food. My mother would do her utmost to ensure this, taking in washing, doing work on the local farms such as cleaning, picking potatoes, scaring crows and so on. One of my earliest recollections is sitting at the side of a field whilst my mother worked, and getting a ride home on the back of a cart-horse in the evening.

When I was very young I can remember only one Christmas present; this was from a lodger named Mr. Sorrell who gave each of us children a dancing spider on springs. These were hung on the wall and joggled up and down; we kept them for years.

My mother was very religious; I think Church-going was a kind of escapism from the background she was in. We went to church every Sunday and we never missed. I was in the choir for seven or eight years. My father rarely went to church, perhaps once or twice a year at Harvest Festival and Christmas. It was an effort to get him into a collar and tie. We had a small church, the gift of Lord Hatherton who occasionally attended with his wife. We had a priest visiting us from Cannock and he was changed frequently. It was a small church probably seating about forty people; there were two lots of choir stalls for about ten boys and about ten men. We had a pipe-organ and the organist was also the choirmaster. I couldn't read music but this probably inspired me to want to, and this is still one of my interests.

Once I had left school and was working I began to think for myself about religion. I walked out in the evening and looked at the stars; I started reading widely and the essays of T. H. Huxley made a great impression on me. Organized religion seemed to be out of touch with, indeed quite remote from, the world and the universe. I had been confirmed, but I left the Church and am now only partially attached and have no great need for organized church religion. However I have never been irreligious and have a profound belief in God.

It was in 1926 that I left school, just after one of the coal strikes. My father had had an accident in the pit; he had been buried by a fall of rock and had dislocated a knee. In a way this was a godsend for he was incapacitated and 'on the box', receiving compensation pay, otherwise he would also have been on strike. All my years at school, my father had been going off to work at seven in the morning and coming back at four in the afternoon filthy with coal dust and almost too tired to wash himself down in the sink. He spent the evenings tired out, reading and smoking; at the week-ends he occasionally got drunk. He never had a holiday away from home all his life until the Miners' Welfare sent him to Weston-super-Mare after his accident. This seemed a bleak kind of life to me. As far as I was concerned I was going to do all in my power to avoid it.

When I left school my father asked me to start to work at the pit but when I told him I would not unless he ordered me to do so, he said simply that I had to get a job somewhere and quickly. I tried to get into the engineering department at the pit but it was clear that there I had to follow my father. For a few weeks I cycled for miles looking for work and eventually with the help of the headmaster, heard of a job at the Gas Company in Cannock and was taken on at ten shillings a week. The work consisted of helping an older collector to read gas-meters and to empty them of money. This job I did for two years. In a way it was not a bad job for it took me into the fresh air, walking five to six miles a day; I saw the insides of many houses, some good and some bad, and I began to be aware of other people and their problems. But best of all I was finishing at four o'clock, not particularly tired or dirty and the evenings were free for night-school.

Night-school seemed to offer one way out of the circumstances. I was fortunate in a way, for the year I left school, the Headmaster had started classes on three evenings a week; these were part of the extension work of the Cannock Chase Mining College then centred in Hednesford four miles away. We studied English, Mathematics and Science and there were only about eight or ten of us. This went on until the Easter examination; I still have the certificate I received. Just before the classes closed at Easter, we were visited by the Principal of the College, Mr. Richard Payne; he was then a young man and had been recently appointed. He told us about opportunities ahead and during the summer I cycled off to Hednesford in the evenings to some special classes and started Chemistry, Physics and French. The novelty for me was to meet people really interested in what I was doing. As a result of this I was allowed to miss the second junior year and went into the senior year at Hednesford in September 1927. I found the studies stimulating, did very well and when a new college building was erected in Cannock shortly afterwards, I was taken on the staff as a Laboratory Assistant at fifteen shillings a week; then I was sixteen years old and started to pay insurance contributions. Apart from the Principal, there were three of four lecturers on the staff and I had all sorts of jobs to do gradually developing interests in the equipment in the engineering and chemistry laboratories. For example I remember analysing rock, effluent and gas samples for the local collieries. I could not spend enough time studying and Mr. Payne did more for me than anybody. Looking back he was a paternal figure for most of the students, me in particular; he never married and his whole life was centred on that College. He would for example spend all day long on the Sundays, working and reading ostensibly, but really to make meals for me whilst I studied. It was he who first gave me the idea of going on to University and indeed while I was studying many engineering subjects in the Advanced Courses, he started a matriculation course which I attended. We took five subjects English, French, Mathematics, Physics and Mechanics and by the time I was eighteen I was the first from the class to take and pass the examinations of London University; I still had no grant or scholarship to go on to a university.

However I had a kind of qualification and began to teach some of the junior classes in the evenings as well as doing my normal job. The County Education Committee provided an avenue to the University in the form of Major Scholarships, two being in Engineering. For the next two years, in my spare time and mostly on my own, I studied for London Intermediate Science in Pure Mathematics, Applied Mathematics, Physics and Chemistry and for the Major Engineering Scholarship in Mathematics, Mechanical Engineering and Electrical Engineering. When I was twenty I got both and went off to the University of Birmingham. Mr. Payne was undoubtedly the man who guided and encouraged me; he has remained one of my greatest friends and influences.

My mother was delighted by my University opportunity but my father remained unaffected in any way, looking upon what

I was doing without envy or pride. He could not be concerned with other people and saw everything in a personal way, scrupulously honouring all his commitments but wishing to be beholden to no one, including me. My mother was glad because she had always considered herself to be in an environment to which she was alien and here was proof at last that she came from a better kind of life. Some aspects of life in Huntington were pretty desperate, husbands and wives having violent rows with blows, furniture broken up and thrown outside in Saturday-night brawls. I remember seeing a man with his arm gashed across by his wife with a knife, and grown men fighting on Sundays; really shattering things for young children to see. I remember a neighbour's daughter who was a prostitute going off for days on end with lorry drivers, and I remember one man having a child by his own daughter and being forced to leave the village. No wonder that my mother, who had come from a quiet village, felt alien.

During my school years, I spent all my holidays in Kingswinford with my aunt, uncle and sister. That was like an escape to paradise for me. My aunt had the family photographs and used to tell me about the Cadman family, that my grandfather and Sir John Cadman's father were brothers. The brothers had some small outcropping pit in South Staffordshire where my grandfather was killed; his brother moved into North Staffordshire. His son, Sir John Cadman was Professor of Mining at Birmingham and later became Baron Silverdale. My aunt used to tell me that education was one way of social improvement and that I could do just as well as the other Cadmans. She also talked of a Dr. Cadman, a theologian who emigrated to Canada. By the time I went to Birmingham, Sir John Cadman had already left and I have never met him. I remember seeing a photograph of him in the Hednesford Technical College and thinking that with a saxon nose and brown eyes I was very much like him facially. Perhaps it was all wishful thinking.

Before I got to Birmingham, I had had two years of self study and when I sat down to lectures, with boys from grammar-schools, I remember it was with a great sense of relief that there were some very able people going to plan the next three or four years for me and all I had to do was respond. The course was in Electrical Engineering. I had really wanted to read Mathematics but the award being in Engineering the education authorities would not allow me to change. I took Electrical Engineering as about the nearest subject to Mathematics I could do and I have never regretted it. The subject has a largely mathematical content; it allows scope for the imagination, and suited me very well. My grant was £100 per annum, but the University also awarded me a free-place reserved for somebody from Staffordshire. My background probably secured this. Anyway it left me £100 clear of fees.

At first I lived in lodgings near the University and I did not like it very much. I found I was not getting along with my studies as well as I wanted. My mother was sorry I was not at home, so I went back and travelled in from Cannock by train, one-and-twopence daily. I took sandwiches with me for lunch. Being at home in the evenings I started teaching one or two classes a week at the college and would earn about fifteen shillings a night.

We were never so well off at home; I had a new bicycle, we bought a piano on instalments at seven shillings and sixpence a month; we got new furniture; we still lived in Huntington though we had moved to a new colliery house. In my years as an undergraduate the only relief from study I allowed myself was to play 'soccer'. One day a week, Wednesday or Saturday, we would be playing away from the University, with the first team. In this way I met students from other departments, Chemistry, Medicine, Dentistry, French, Education and so on. Mostly while we were travelling, often long distances by train, we talked of all sorts of topics and this I found to be a really broadening influence. I was ultimately captain of the team and at one time earlier, even thought of professional football as a career.

My elder sister died a few weeks before I took my final examination and how I managed to get a first-class honours degree I don't know, for I was greatly affected and in a frightful state. After graduation, Mr. Payne wanted me to join the College staff as a lecturer at a quite attractive salary of five pounds per week. I didn't want to do this and felt guilty about it, particularly as he had really done so much for me. The depression had been on. There were not many good offers from industry, a typical one being thirty-five shillings per week as a graduate apprentice. During vacations I had been working in the Electrical department of the local colliery, and also with a Wolverhampton firm and though I did consider it I refused an offer from the latter firm to go into their mercury-arc department. However my problems were solved for some time by Professor Cramp asking me to stay on to do research work at Birmingham. This appealed to me and I stayed on with a Bowen engineering scholarship of £120 a year and a £25 grant from the Miners Welfare Fund to which my father had contributed. I carried on travelling and teaching in the evenings, and playing football.

To move nearer the station in 1936, I started to buy a new house in Cannock, through a Building Society. My mother and I had great difficulty in persuading my father to move there. It meant he had to travel three miles by bus apart from going against his principles. By the Easter of 1938 I had completed the experimental work of my research on iron under Dr. Greig, now professor at King's College London. We read papers to the British Association in Nottingham and in Cambridge.

In Easter 1938, despite regulations, I was allowed to leave the University and take up an appointment as Assistant Engineer in the Post Office at some £300 per annum, the best appointment financially then available. This meant moving down to London and I worked in the Telegraph division of the Research Station at Dollis Hill. In the summer of 1938 I wrote up my Ph.D. thesis and graduated in the following November.

I was in the Post Office until war broke out. It had been evident in the Civil Service that war was imminent and the long-term work I was doing had been scheduled to close down. I was moved to the Portsmouth area to work with the local telephone manager. I was only there for a few weeks for I had already volunteered for the R.N.V.R. and was called up in October as a Sub-Lieutenant in the newly-formed Electrical Branch. The work I was concerned with was on underwater equipment for detecting submarines. The next six years, I spent in various appointments, Scotland, Ceylon, London and finished as a Lieutenant-Commander in January 1946 when I was demobilized.

After demobilization I was committed to return to the Post Office but on going back for interview it was clear that after an absence of six years, I was regarded as of less use to them than before; in fact I was to be reinstated on a probationary basis. Instead of returning there, I accepted an appointment as a Senior Scientific Officer of the British Iron and Steel Research Association whose director was Sir Charles Goodeve whom I had known in the Navy. It meant working in London, however, and this did not suit me or my wife, a Lancashire girl whom I married in 1940. We were both keen mountaineers. We therefore moved to Glasgow in October 1946 when I took an appointment as lecturer at the University, working under the late Professor Hague. I spent eight years there before coming to Nottingham as Head of Department in 1954.

Looking back on my educational career, my beginnings always seem to be with me; I feel they are a background which can never be shaken off. I don't sit around regretting this background and often I draw inspiration from it. The way I approach things is conditioned by the way I was forced to approach them then. The size of a task rarely causes me to worry; the effort required I make with a sort of determination based on experience.

My background has affected me socially; that is not to say I go round deploring the fact that my father was a coal-miner or, by inverted snobbery, glorying in it. I sometimes feel I would have liked a cultured background, drawing-room talk of books, music, the arts. I don't talk with the ease a lot of other people do in company, and readily retire into my own thoughts unless somebody jerks me out of them.

If there is a lower middle-class, this is probably what I am in my approach to things. Naturally I wanted to give my son and daughter all the things I had missed and to my astonishment I find that neither of them particularly wants them. For example, I took my son when he was young to one of the Public Schools and told him I would like him to go there. He took one look and said he didn't want to go and seems even now not to have regretted his choice. In this environment I would have wanted to go to Cambridge but he never even wanted to make the effort. He is now at one of the new universities. My daughter is at the local College of Further Education. There are many values worth preserving in working-class life; the drive and energy, the independence and the integrity. These I got from my father though he never tried to inculcate anything in anybody. My father when he was once out of a job walked from Kingswinford up to Middlesbrough; few would do anything comparable nowadays.

Times have changed radically and I am glad to see so many young people getting the educational opportunity to make the best of their abilities. I think Britain is right to do what it is now doing, to open wide the doors for everybody with ability to go as far as they can. Whether this will have the one-to-one effect on service to the community that it ought to have I am not so convinced. My comparative success has meant that I have been able to remove the harshness of the economic pressure from my children's background. Britain with mounting debts is busy doing this on a national scale; the relative ease of acquiring educational opportunities may lead to these being undervalued, particularly as no sense of obligation is involved. As a nation we are committed; those with integrity will respond to the opportunities created, and honour their obligation. I hope there are enough of them.

XI

ARNOLD WESKER[1]

Playwright

I was born on Empire Day, 1932 which was May 24th. I was born in a place where most Jews were born. I suspect if you go back to all the well-known Jews in the country asking them where they were born it would be the same place, a Jewish maternity home called Mother Levi's in Underwood Street which is just off the Whitechapel Road. It is now a pukka Jewish maternity home in Stoke Newington, a very good one. For the first two or three years, my parents lived in a number of streets in the East End. I can't remember which streets they were and certainly can't remember at first-hand having lived there.

My first recollection of the East End is living in Fashion Street, one of a number of streets named after the Huguenots, like Weaver Street and Threadneedle Street. Fashion Street is a narrow street joining up Commercial Street and Brick Lane, that part of Commercial Street where Spitalfields Church is. On the other side, across Commercial Street from Fashion Street you walk, more or less, into Spitalfields Market. Fashion Street, together with Flower and Dean Street, which was the next street along, running parallel, was where my grandfather, my father's mother, and his sisters, my aunts, lived in buildings ironically named after one of the Rothschilds—Rothschild Buildings. There was a very interesting playground inside Roths-child Buildings, the place where I remember playing. That playground incidentally was structurally arresting, because the buildings form a square and contained within the square is this

[1] Transcribed from a recorded conversation with the editor.

playground, and I am always taking friends to see this, and it's very dramatic. It's like inside Sing-Sing prison, but I loved it, despite the fact that it's dirty, it's mean and it's got a stone floor. The principle of people in a block facing or backing on to each other so that the kids knew, played together and were friends, is a good principle. So those are the three areas I remember.

Fashion Street consists of a number of houses, nearly all of which have shops on the ground floor and basements, and then you go up stone stairs and there are landings, and there are two rooms on each landing and a lavatory on the half-landing. It was a three-storey tenement block and we lived on the top floor. There were the two rooms and the landing, and the kitchen was on the landing. The two rooms were about fifteen feet by thirty feet. They were attic rooms, of course, very much like my present study. I think, because of that, I have always loved attic rooms. One was a combined living-room, dining-room and bedroom with a folding bed where my parents slept, and the other was a bedroom where my sister and I slept. The rooms were always filled with people, constantly coming and going.

Apart from mother and father there was my sister and myself. She was eight years older and she went to Spitalfields Foundation School, across the road. It was a very 'posh' school, with very high standards. It is, incidentally, where I imagine I got my own accent from, through her, and I've always had this, and no one has ever believed that I could have possibly spent all my youth in the East End and speak like this. In fact, people in the East End, even at the time I remember, always used to say to my mother, 'Is that your son?', I suppose because of this strange accent with which I spoke. My sister was a very bright girl and got to Spitalfields by winning a scholarship. Before that she went to the local elementary school, just down the road.

One important event during those early years was that we were evacuated. I was evacuated with my sister and her school to Ely. She didn't stay on to take matriculation which upset my mother, because my sister was a member of the Young Communist League and she felt her responsibility was to aid

176

the war. So she left school and went into armaments, and then finally to book-keeping. But she had met the man who was to be her husband in the Young Communist League. At seventeen she was married to him, when he was nineteen, and then he went into the Air Force and spent about three or four years abroad and came back, and they are happily married with three children.

My brother-in-law influenced me greatly. He was a wood-worker, a carpenter, and worked in the building trade, but reared on the early Socialists he always wanted to become a furniture-maker, to make his own furniture by hand. They subsequently went away to Norfolk and he tried to set up as a furniture-maker and he lived there for eleven years, I think. Now he has returned to London—he couldn't make a go of it—and has gradually built up a small business, making sometimes individual pieces of furniture, but doing interiors and restaurants and banks and so on, generally hating the work he is doing.

Father was a Russian, Mother a Transylvanian. I deduce that my paternal grandfather was religious. I say this because I seem to remember my father constantly saying how learned his father was, how he was able to recite the *Torah* and the scriptures, and so I see him as a religious man. I also know that he was a revolutionary and in Russia, in those days, was among those who formed one of the first Trade Unions in Dneipepetrovsk. They even say there's a plaque up with his name on it. I would love to see this because I remember him. My parents came to this country when my mother was about thirteen and my father about eleven years old. My father must have come to Britain about 1910 and mother about 1912. My mother's people came to London and my father's people came to Swansea. There are many of my relatives still in Swansea, uncles and aunts who have a Welsh accent.

My paternal grandfather, I remember as being blind. I remember him coming round the corner from Flower and Dean Street to Fashion Street up to us to eat this dish of Matza—it's a special thing you do with Matza, you dip into egg and fry, and I remember him being kindly and getting on very well with my mother. My mother was very fond of him. She was not so fond of my father's mother, who I also remember as being bed-ridden most of the time, in Flower and Dean Street, and being looked after by two aunts. My paternal grandfather was a tailor and so my father was a tailor, that is, they were tailor's machinists. My father certainly hated his work. My mother was also a tailor's machinist, but sometimes a cook in a kitchen. Her father was what we call a *Shoicket*, the religious man who slaughtered the chickens. I didn't know my mother's parents at all, but they were of Jewish peasant stock. It is difficult to say what motives brought both families to Britain. They were most probably fleeing from the pogroms. Actually, we all say our parents were fleeing from pogroms since it has a somewhat romantic sound. But perhaps the word had just got round that England was a great place, like America, and it was part of a general movement.

Two things about my parents were that in addition to being Jewish they were Communists, and also Atheists. But they were Jews who, although they acknowledged Judaism as their own cultural heritage, mirrored the big problem and dilemma of the Jew in the Diaspora. What is a Jew? A Jew is a Jew is a Jew, and is made such by a whole knowledge of his past and a whole mass of mannerisms and attitudes, many of which at some level are linked up with the religious aspects of Judaism. All these have gone to make a certain kind of human being, so that I recognize myself obviously to be a Jew without any great knowledge of the Jewish religion. I think my attitudes are very Jewish. A play like 'Roots', even though it is about Norfolk farm-labourers is Jewish. And so I think they were Jewish in this way and it very much affected the way in which they were Communists as well. I think it was all part of a Messianic vision of the good life that was always there to be had. The Communist framework was an intellectual as well as an emotional framework for my parents. There was constant ideological discussion at home, argument and disputation all the time.

So all this affected my parents' attitude to education. It wasn't ever a question of, 'Now you must study', and 'Education is a good thing because it is necessary to be a lawyer and get on', but it was the common currency of day-to-day living that ideas were discussed round the table, and it was taken for granted that there were books in the house and that we would read. These were mostly political books and the novels of Jack London, Sinclair Lewis, of Tolstoy and Gorki. I began later to discover other authors for myself, but it wasn't until I came under the influence of my sister and brother-in-law that I discovered Balzac and de Maupassant and a whole range of literature. My brother-in-law was a great influence and a sort of hero to me.

The schools I went to were Jewish infant-schools, Commercial Street School, Deal Street, all in the area, and Christchurch, which was a school in Brick Lane run by nuns or monks, and mine was a very ordinary education. I just wasn't very good. I was a very bad student. I had intelligence and was obviously bright, but I didn't have the ability to really study. I suppose I wasn't interested in most of the things they tried to teach me. I have really only ever been good at the things I have been interested in. That is to say, I was interested in Maths and so was good at Maths and at typing; but I wasn't interested in Science and so I wasn't good at it. I was constantly playing truant and spent a great deal of time in leading gangs, and in fights and would not apply myself seriously to 'getting-on'. I was acceptable to many adults, because I had a certain attractive cheekiness which got me by.

In 1939 I was evacuated with my sister's school to Ely, and stayed there for a short while. My sister as I noted came back to work in munitions and I was left in Ely until 1940, but after that I nagged my way back to London. I can remember that during the period of the entire war the following things happened: I was evacuated to Ely, came back to London, evacuated to Buckingham, came back to London, evacuated to Devon, came back to London, evacuated to South Wales, came back to London. I remember vividly some of the people I met. In addition, during that period, we also changed from living in Stepney to living in Hackney, so that added to the environmental change, schools were constantly changing, and people too. I suppose the net result of all this moving about was that I discovered that there was more to England than London. I began to develop a sense of the countryside. I can't consciously remember thinking at the time, 'I am making a discovery', but in retrospect obviously I was.

The emotional climate of my family life was interesting. My mother was a very easily recognizable Jewish matriarchal head of the family; most Jewish mothers are heads of the family. It is assumed that the men are. I mean, they have a way of letting the men seem to be, but of course, the women are in control. And she was a great loyal, beautiful, responsible, and very gay person whose gayness was soured over the years, because my father was a highly intelligent and a very charming, attractive personality, but he hated work. One never knows whether he really hated work itself or whether he just hated the work he was doing. As a human being he was very sensitive and this comes into conflict with my mother's sense of duty and responsibility. Regardless of how much a man hated his work he had a responsibility to his family. This caused a great deal of conflict which took place when I was between the age of five and nine or ten. My sister was between thirteen and seventeen—in her adolescence—and this affected her much more than it did me.

Even though there were quarrels, and even though there was real poverty, in missing meals and then having fish-and-chips, and I had to sell my stamp collection at one time because there was no money, despite all this I do not remember it as being a period of hardship or being miserable or unhappy. When I talked to my mother, for instance, of how marvellous it was in those days she would say, 'What are you talking about, marvellous? They were unclean, terrible days.' Neither does my sister remember it as being a happy period.

The change to Hackney made a lot of differences to my environment. There were more rooms. We lived in a block of L.C.C. flats. They were terrible flats, now I think about it. My mother still lives there, on the third floor with iron railings, but there were four rooms, and a separate kitchen, and I had a bedroom to myself. There was a bath in the kitchen, and there was a bloody great big boiler in the corner. I can remember when we first moved there, we fed it with coal. The lunacy of Borough Engineers or architects to build like this is incredible, and I leaned back in the bath and burned my back

180

because the boiler was right against the bath. We finally got rid of it. Compared with Fashion Street it was a palace, and Upper Clapton Road was a great, wide road and round the corner was Springfield Park. Springfield Park was a pilgrimage for us when we were living in Stepney and here we were living five minutes away from it.

The move was only seven or eight miles, but most of the Jews who were in Stepney, moved out to Clapton, Hackney, Stanford Hill, Stoke Newington and that area, and the next stage was to Golder's Green, Finchley, Swiss Cottage, Hampstead and then the counties, mainly Surrey. And so we were part of this pattern, we moved from Stepney out into Hackney. For me there was much more space, more greenery, all the difference of moving from a slum to a residental area of a different kind. I can't remember anything about my first schools although I know exactly where they are. The only image I have is an obscene image of all of us youngsters lying on the floor during P.T., physical-training exercises, stretching our necks to look up the skirts of one of the teachers as she passed by. My reaction to formal education was normal, I think. Get away whenever one could; play truant. I don't, though, have any extraordinary violent hates about school, nor can I remember loving it passionately. All my emotional memories of those years come really from my home.

I must have been at the local primary or elementary school until the age of eleven. I took an examination which I failed, but I was obviously bright and they had to do something with me, and so they recommended me for what was then known as a Central School. Not a Grammar-School where one learned Latin, but a Central school were one was trained in book-keeping, shorthand and typing. This was Upton House school for boys, where I stayed until I was sixteen. At the end of my time at Upton House I took the Oxford School Certificate and failed. But my most vivid memories of school are, I suppose, of Upton House, and they are really vivid memories. I remember enormous snowball fights on a bomb-site that were held between our school and another school. These grew into great campaigns when every lunch hour we would form up in organized battalions at one end of the bomb-site, which was enormous, and the other school came to the other end and we would begin throwing snowballs. It was all just great until they began putting stones in the snowballs, and then it became nasty. I remember the fads, the exchange of comics, the collecting of cigarette cards, the phases of pitch-and-toss. Going back to the elementary school, I know what I can remember, not having school dinners and pocketing the money my mother gave me for the week and buying cigarette cards.

Regarding the work done at school, I can remember I was interested in writing, having written my first poem at the age of twelve for the wrong reasons. My brother-in-law wrote poetry, short-stories and essays, and I was so passionate about him I wanted to please him, so I wrote this poem, which is a terrible, terrible poem and it certainly wasn't written because I wanted to write. It was a poem called 'The Breeze'. It isn't worth thinking about, but it released something and I discovered I wanted to write, that I wanted to write poetry, and it then began to pour out. Sometimes I wrote three or four poems a day. I changed from having written the poem in order to please someone to writing poetry because I wanted to. Yes, and also I remember writing essays and getting high marks for them, and I think this was because I did imaginative things with those dreary titles schoolmasters always give you, which incidentally did me well during the period at school, but was my undoing for the matriculation, because whereas my English master understood what I was doing, the examiners didn't take too kindly to what I did with their suggested titles. So with my English I just got a pass instead of a credit. This was the one result which nearly brought tears to my eyes.

I didn't even bother to take Science for the matriculation as I was obviously so bad at it. I took French, History, Geography and Maths. I was very good at Maths. I remember the response of my English master to my essays. He encouraged me and indulged me. He was a great cynic—he made great fun of me because I could never spell, and I had really no sense of grammar, and I misused words. Up until recently I used to come in after going a long day without food and rub my hands and say things like, 'God, I'm ravishing'. Even recently, in the new play I had written, instead of saying 'gangrenous' I said 'gangerous'.

But this English teacher indulged the imaginative side of me and for this I was eternally grateful. I remember a French master whom I loved because he was a very gentle man. I remember cheating in my second year in Geometry and coming top and from then on having to be good in Geometry. Because of that I developed a great passion for Geometry and was always good in Geometry as well as Maths. Generally I think I enjoyed Maths and Geometry because of the order they conveyed. This isn't unusual. I think the opposing distinctions made very often between the scientist and the artist are nonsense, and I responded to the kind of logic and order that there is in Geometry in the same way as I enjoy confronting a new book I am going to write the next play in and marshalling and ordering all those things I am going to use.

I was never very good at French, although I always had a good accent, and I imagine this was so because I didn't understand English grammar. I just don't know how the English language is made up. If someone talks to me about tenses and past participles I wouldn't know what they would be talking about. I think this is the reason why I am a bad linguist because I don't know how the English language is made up. I couldn't ever find the corresponding words, but when finally I went to live in France—I worked there for nine months as a cook— I began to talk the language very well. And now I find I speak French sufficiently to enable me to converse with foreigners who come to live here.

The major subjects that excited me were English, Mathematics and History. I think I tolerated the kind of history they taught in schools because it was necessary. But I really enjoyed history through the novels I read and the Lytton Stracheys and the incidental history one gets from biographies and literature. I was very good at typing because I wanted to type. I was terrible at shorthand; I could never remember the outlines. I was reasonably good at book-keeping because I enjoyed figures and those lovely lines. Perhaps I didn't respond to Science because we had such a bloody awful master, a really terrible master.

Then I was expelled at fourteen or fifteen. It was a temporary expulsion. It was all because I had a row with the schoolmistress who taught us Geography and who took us for typing and shorthand. She was a very strange lady. One evening, I didn't want to stay in for typing. Our typing lessons were after normal school hours and I could never really understand why this was, but it was, and one evening I just didn't want to stay. I knew I was good at typing so it didn't worry me and so I went to her and said, 'Look, I've got to go and have a hair cut.' It was a lie, but I told her I wanted to go and have a hair cut and she said, 'No, you can't.' I said, 'Look, don't be silly. I must have this hair cut.' And she said, 'No, you can't,' and I said, 'I will go and bring you a note tomorrow,' and she said, 'No, you won't,' and I said, 'Yes, I will,' and she said, 'No, you won't,' and I said, 'I'm going,' and she said, 'You'll sit there until I decide.' It was a battle of personalities. So I sat there and did nothing until she said, 'All right, you can go; I will report you to the headmaster tomorrow.' And, of course, there were a series of other incidents in the past for which I was hauled up at one time or another. The headmaster raged into the Science room that morning and said, 'Wesker, pack your books and go.' And I can remember with trembling legs inwardly, but seeming very, very calm outwardly, I walked right past him, and he called me back and said, 'Are you going to apologize? You know you can apologize or you can go.' So I said I was going. I packed up my books and one by one went to the masters and said, 'I've been expelled,' and left.

Then the headmaster did a very silly thing. We had a Jewish master who came to give us Religious Instruction and also took casual Maths classes. And the headmaster thought it would be politic to send this Jewish master round to see Wesker and his parents and wean him back, since it was a very feeble thing he had expelled me for. So the Jewish master came—he was not part of the established staff and I had no great affection for him—and he said to my mother, 'Look, we're Jews, we are tolerated, we are visitors in this land and occasionally,' he said, 'it's necessary to eat humble pie.' That was the last thing he should have said to my mother who screamed, 'What are you talking about?' and he was dismissed, sent packing. I finally did go back because it was all very silly and I went back on my own terms, I suppose, after only a few days away.

ARNOLD WESKER

Taking the School Certificate was really just to complete
my schooling and, of course, I failed. I got a distinction in
Maths and a credit in History. I think I failed Geography but
that shouldn't have been. A lot of us failed Geography that
time because we had all read a question in the same way and
apparently it was wrong. And I was awarded a pass in English
subjects, nothing in Science and a credit in commercial subjects, and I think just a bare pass in French. These were not
enough to get me a School Certificate. When that was done I
couldn't have stayed any longer at that school. I don't think
there was the machinery to go forward on to Grammar-School.
I suppose the object was to go forward simply with credits,
with honours, out into the big world to claim a job, as indeed
our top boy did, as an official on the Metropolitan Water Board,
a white collar job.

For myself, I wanted to be a writer. I also wanted to act and
so I tried to get into the Royal Academy of Dramatic Art. I
passed the R.A.D.A. entrance test, but I failed to get an L.C.C.
scholarship. So I said, 'Right, I can't act, I must learn a living.
If I'm going to write, I'm going to write whatever I do anyway.
The living I earn must be in a field where there is something
rewarding; what else could it be but what my brother-in-law
did? I would become a furniture maker, deal in live materials,
wood.' And so I did and that lasted for six months and I became
redundant and then I went into the building trade, still staying in wood, as a carpenter's mate, and then came a series of
jobs over a period of time, including a job as a bookseller's
assistant. The book-selling didn't do anything for me other than
give me access to books, which I could buy at a cheaper rate.
I never read quickly, but I read hungrily. Reading was a real
need, and at a crisis in my life when I was in the R.A.F. reading
became almost a physical need. At one time I think I got
through three D. H. Lawrence novels in a weekend.

My writing continued from the age of twelve. I constantly
wrote poems and short stories and once I'd left school I continued writing short stories and poems. The only time I wrote
a novel was when I was in the R.A.F. The novel from the
R.A.F. was never published. It isn't a good novel but the
chapters in that novel became the basis for the scenes in 'Chips

with Everything'. The short stories were never published either. There was a single poem in a Jewish magazine, and that was all. I became interested in writing plays because of my interest in wanting to be an actor and because I belonged to an amateur dramatic group. I wrote one play when I came out of the Air Force for this amateur dramatic group, which the person who ran the drama group didn't like, so I didn't seriously consider writing plays professionally. I did nothing with it. I didn't really think I was a dramatist: I had simply belonged to a drama group and had written a play for them.

Then I went to Paris and worked in the kitchen. On this job I saved up some money and decided I wanted very much to write and direct films. It was the cinema which influenced me as a creative person. More precisely, it was the cinema which gave me my sense of drama more than the theatre. And so I saved up this money and came to study at the London School of Film Technique. Then a series of things happened. Ken Tynan came to the *Observer* as drama critic, and inaugurated his period there by setting up a drama competition for which I wrote a play called 'The Kitchen', just because it was a competition. It didn't get anywhere because the play was too short. Tynan has subsequently told me it was too short and this had been why the panel dismissed it. Then I saw 'Look Back In Anger' and somehow this triggered something off in me, and I felt the Theatre was somewhere where something could happen, and so I wrote 'Chicken Soup with Barley' and I knew when I had written 'Chicken Soup with Barley' that I had, at last, written something.

My wife is the daughter of Norfolk farm-labourers, who are still farm-labourers. Her brother is a farm-labourer and one of her sisters is the wife of a farm-labourer; another is the wife of a garage mechanic. She herself went to an ordinary elementary school and left at fourteen, and then went away to work as a waitress. Education was really non-existent and I suppose her intelligence and instinct and intuitiveness really began to flower when it came into contact with London, with my family and the growing circle of friends which I was discovering. The world only slowly makes sense to me; I only understand things gradually, and because of this I found my wife and I, despite the fact that the habit of self-education was stronger in me, were able to make many discoveries together.

Looking back, I don't know what were the important ingredients in my background in helping me to express emotion and feeling. I can only point to obvious things like the emotionalism that's inherently Jewish. I think I happened to have been born the kind of person that really wanted to share, to discuss things, so that everything I came into touch with, and was exposed to, I had to talk about, to tell people about. I wanted to ask questions, and if you have this need in you to forge a language you reach out for everything that's available, you reach out to the language not only of the books but also the comics you read.

The landmarks of my formative years are fairly simple, apart from obvious personalities like mother, father, brother-in-law and sister. I think a book like 'Mort D'Arthur', which I can remember reading ten or twelve times, must somewhere have been a great shaping influence. The whole Jewish political atmosphere of the house, the contact in the Young Communist League I had, the short period of time that I was in it, but even more important than that was my period in the Zionist Movement when I was thirteen years old, where one developed a sense of comradeship and ability to do things together. That was during the period of living in Hackney, and I must have belonged to it until I was about sixteen. It was a Zionist group known as the Builders. And it was like many Zionist groups in the country, designed to attract Jewish children and get them used to the idea of Israel as a Jewish home, with the purpose of bringing them to Israel. I never got that far, but many of my friends did and are there. But the idealism behind 'Habonim' linked with the idealism behind the Communist party, together with that part of the Jewish personality that passionately cares—some parts of the Jewish personality are of course utterly bankrupt of any kind concern—are all what have made me the person I am. Although God knows if anyone is ever capable of knowing what makes them what they are.

Looking at my education, my formal education, I endured it rather than enjoyed it. It was the peripheral things, apart from the English and Maths, which gave me pleasure and meaning. Regarding my own children, I must confess to a certain fear that a formal education will damage them. I don't know and I think one must play it by ear and just not apply pressures and not talk about how they must go to university or they must do anything. The Stuart Halls and the Richard Hoggarts who survive university life are few and far between. One meets students who are themselves sort of alive and interesting and nice and good, but I suspect that university higher education does not on the whole produce a real human being, it produces a component part of society.

POSTSCRIPT

The eleven chapters which have formed this book have not in any way been intended as a typical sample of the population. There has been little attempt to sample those who could be numbered as successful in either higher education or through vocational achievement. I suppose, however, that in selecting these eleven essays out of many, there has emerged a kind of illustration of achievement. The ages of the people have ranged from over sixty-five to those just under thirty years of age and they have stemmed from working-class backgrounds in Sheffield, Wales, Cumberland, Manchester, Yorkshire, the Midlands, London and Glasgow. Practically all of the contributors have originated from working-class backgrounds. I have included Sir Gerald Nabarro as one interesting exception where a boy born into a middle-class situation had declined through bankruptcy, as one was so easily able to do in those days, into working-class poverty. It is significant, perhaps, that there are only two women out of the eleven contributors, for I found it very easy to find men who had fought their way up through the educational system or outside the educational system, but very few women.

It is extremely difficult to generalize about the breakthroughs narrated in this book. Some generalizations, however, are possible when one sees that most of the contributors attributed to luck that they met certain particular people at certain times in their career. With Arnold Wesker it was his brother-in-law, with Richard Hoggart it was two Headmasters and an outstanding Professor of English, but in almost every case there was a key person who somehow brought out the latent talent or who awoke ambition at a particularly important phase of life.

From the small number of cases put forward, the drive of an ambitious mother, sometimes seeking an escape for her children from the drab working-class situation which she faces, is very obvious. It is this mother's drive which has been responsible

189

for Jane Mitchell, for Sheila Fell, for Derek Davies and many others who have fought their way upwards through education or through vocational talent. It is obvious that the role of the home and the attitudes to education evinced by people like Douglas do play a very important part. For some the school exerts a great influence and for others seems to have exerted no influence whatever. Arnold Wesker's school was really that of the kitchen and the workman's bench. For Nabarro, his school was basically the Army, and it is interesting to see that the enlargement of experience beyond the school, through the Army, through a Scout Group or through a Youth Club, has been responsible for some of these developing later, and the school seems in their case to have played a minimal role. But with others the school has played a very important role in that there have been teachers of genius or people who have known how to pump information in such a way that it can be retained for the jumping of the necessary educational hurdles to be faced. Three who came through a conventional grammar-school into higher education, Jane Mitchell, Denis Marsden and Richard Hoggart, all in fact confess to not knowing what education was about until rather late in their achievements. They were so busy doing what they were told and following the excitement of receiving information that they were ill-prepared to think for themselves.

There are in these pages some interesting observations to which teachers and intending teachers should pay close attention. Professor Allaway, for example, saying because he was small, poorly-dressed and having a working-class speech, he was overlooked by a certain teacher. Teachers themselves who belong basically to a middle-class grouping or want to think of themselves as such, often tend to look down upon the working-class child, to minimize his potential and not to realize it even when it is very evident. And yet men like Professor Henton Davies remember how enjoyable it was being read to by his primary-school teacher and how stimulating most of these people found their schooling when there was anyone with imagination to bring them out.

Some of these chapters read as though they belong to a quite different generation, but the Plowden Report (1967) spells

190

it out once again that this country, as America and many other countries, still continues to produce a large number of people who come through the cycle of poverty unable to break through and continuing the poverty circle in their own children. These have poor attitudes to education, no concept of what education should be about, and even in an affluent society seem intent on begetting poverty factors among their own children and their children's children. There are many hundreds of thousands of children in schools and Educational Priority Areas, many like those in which the Allaways, the Hoggarts, the Davies, the Mitchells, the Nabarros, the Weskers of the past were raised who, because they have not had the good luck to meet the right kind of people and because they are in poor schools, remain unstimulated, unable to break out. With some their disadvantage still remains the area to which they belong, the poverty of mal-nourishment not of the body sometimes but the mal-nourishment of the mind, a lack of conversation, a lack of interest in formal education and what its intentions are. If there are lessons to be learned from these breakthroughs it is that the most unlikely backgrounds will yield, where there is purpose, imagination and idealism on the part of some individuals.

When one looks at the authors who have contributed to this book one is asked whether the circumstances in which they were reared were handicaps or in some cases spurs to their endeavours? Certainly Professor Henton Davies was nourished by his background though it did contain several poverty elements. Sheila Fell although apparently coming from a very poor background was nourished artistically, and throughout her own account one can see how her mother's artistry and concern communicated itself to her through shape, form and colour. And so we have one of our leading artists in the country reacting to and often painting elements of what is basically an ugly unproductive area of the countryside in West Cumberland. Has something of the ugliness and yet something of the warmth of the East End of London communicated itself through the writings of Arnold Wesker? Certainly many of the people in this book reacted against their environment and it seems as though their environments created such a threat or such a distaste that like Professor Parton and Dennis Marsden they wanted to

191

escape from the area, and education was one of the ways by which one could take flight.

Success, of course, carries with it certain costs, and many contributors tell of the strains incurred in breaking through the barriers they faced. Estrangement of proud but puzzled relatives appears to be a built-in risk. This may be offset by work habits of a strenuous kind, but these in their way, may also create strain. There are so many imponderables at work in any person's life that it is difficult to differentiate. Yet one thing is clear, that no achievements for these contributors came without struggle, and this struggle, often physical, but mainly social and psychological, was a direct outcome of the environmental and social handicaps they had to overcome. One question to ask is how environments and facilities for leisure, work, housing, and education may be improved in such a way as to act as stimulants to individual efforts. Some social legislation may do quite the opposite.

Since all these events which have been written about have happened, many changes have occurred in education. But one is impelled to ask the question whether in fact we have as yet achieved free universal educational opportunity for all in such a way that those who come from stunted backgrounds are given the fullest opportunity to succeed? These essays, I trust, will show quite convincingly, although not in any statistical manner, that equality of educational opportunity can never be realized until the worst elements of social inequality are removed. The decaying areas of our towns and cities are still those areas which today provide us with our greatest challenge.